MW00783889

The Gun and the Law—Jeffrey Hunter as Temple Houston, 1963. *(Photofest)*

JEFFREY HUNTER
AND TEMPLE HOUSTON

A Story of Network Television

GLENN A. MOSLEY

BearManor
Media

Albany, Georgia

Published in the USA by:
BearManor Media
PO Box 1129
Duncan, OK 73534-1129
www.BearManorMedia.com

ISBN 1-59393-647-8
ISBN-13: 978-1-59393-647-1

Printed in the United States.

Design and Layout by Allan T. Duffin.

Dedication

To

Sheri, my wife

A story herself

Table of Contents

Acknowledgments

Any book that has been percolating for as long as this one has will have a list of helpful people, who, in one way or another, assisted the author along the way. That is certainly true in this case.

In absolutely no order of importance, the author is very grateful to the following people: Jim Meyer, Roger L. Brown, Steven Dhuey, Stephen Macht, Jeanette Macht-Finkelstein, Sari Korman-Hunt, Donna Kentley, Miranda Smith, Mary Packer, Erin Mosley, Joseph Colter, Heather Salter, Jeff Kimberling, Jack Turley, Paul Green, and Kathleen Creeden.

The staffs at the following libraries were very helpful to this project over the years and I am grateful: University of Idaho Library, the Holland Library at Washington State University; UCLA Special Collections; the Warner Bros. Archive at USC; the UCLA Cinema- Television Library; the Wisconsin Center for Film and Theatre Research; the Howard Gottlieb Research Center at Boston University; the Notre Dame Archives; the Occidental College Library; the Merrill Library at Utah State University; and the Lilly Library at Indiana University.

My sincere thanks to everyone at BearManor Media, and to Laura LaPlaca at the Warner Bros. Archive, for your help and interest.

A special hug to the family pets who sat with me over the years, all of whom really knew their nouns and verbs.

And, as always, my parents were there, from beginning to end.

§

Chapter One
The Summer of '63

It was a role that Jack Webb, the head of television at Warner Brothers in 1963, said Jeffrey Hunter was "absolutely right" for.[1]

The role was the lead in *Temple Houston*, a television western being developed at Warner Brothers that year, aimed at a timeslot on NBC-TV sometime in 1964.

Jeffrey Hunter had by this time starred in more than thirty motion pictures, made television and radio appearances, and was well liked. "A sweet man," said actress Marie Windsor. "He was warm and gentle and very talented."[2]

Jeffrey Hunter loved the part. "We did some research on him," Hunter said at the time the pilot was produced, "and he's probably considered one of the finest lawyers in the last part of the 19th Century.

"He was a colorful and eloquent man who dressed like a plantation owner. The show is a different kind of western, a whodunit on horseback. And it has humor in it."[3]

In March, Hunter starred in the pilot for the series, which would focus on the exploits of the real-life attorney Temple Houston, the son of Texas legend Sam Houston.

"He was only three years old when his father died, and a few years afterward his mother died," Hunter said. "In his teens he was a trail hand and a cowpuncher. Then he studied law and passed the bar exams before he was twenty years old. Later he became a district attorney and figured in a number of memorable trials."[4]

It was a role Hunter was excited about, but it wasn't the only good work-related news to come Hunter's way during 1963.

Director John Ford had hired Hunter as the fifth star of his latest western, *The Long Flight*, about the trek of Cheyenne Indians back to their Wyoming homeland from Oklahoma (the film was released in 1964 as *Cheyenne Autumn*). Joining a cast

Jeffrey Hunter as Temple Houston. *(Photofest)*

that already included Richard Widmark, James Stewart, Spencer Tracy, and Carroll Baker, Hunter couldn't help but be excited. This was to be his fourth film with Ford; the others were *The Searchers*, *The Last Hurrah*, and *Sergeant Rutledge*, and they represented some of his best work in films.

But for Jeff Hunter, *The Long Flight* was more than just another film with John Ford. It was to be a major release in 1964, from a major studio, with a big budget, and an A list director—a combination that had eluded the actor since he starred as Jesus in *King of Kings* in 1961.

It wasn't that Hunter had been idle since the worldwide release of *King of Kings*, in 1961 and 1962. Quite the contrary; he had been very busy. But despite the microscope that epic film had been under—or perhaps because of it—Hunter's career following its release had continued much the same as it had since 1956.

But *King of Kings* was a major studio release with a big budget. It was supposed to be the kind of film that gave an actor's big screen career a huge boost, wasn't it?

"It didn't do him any good," production executive Charles B. Fitzsimons said later.[5] Following *King of Kings*, Hunter had been working steadily, was being widely seen, and was popular, in films such as *No Man Is An Island* and *The Longest Day*. He'd also been making a series of impressive television guest appearances in highly-rated series such as *Combat*, *Death Valley Days*, *Checkmate*, and *Alfred Hitchcock Presents*.

"Television," he said, "always offered me a change from the cotton-candy college sophomore things they gave me in pictures."[6]

But where was the next big film? The answer to that question is part of the reason Hunter turned to the role of Temple Houston.

Consistently over the years, Hunter maintained publicly in interviews that the biblical film hadn't hurt, only helped, his career.

In 1963, he said, "Playing Christ has not in any way limited or affected my career. I wanted to do the part…I'm glad I did it…It was a beautiful concept. In an age where there is so much strife, it was a chance to reiterate the basic concept of brotherhood."[7]

In 1964, he said, "The role has only helped me and in no way prejudiced producers in casting me. The week *King of Kings* opened in New York I was playing a role in (*Checkmate*) on T.V."[8]

Friends, though, were left to wonder, even years later. Long-time friend and fellow actor Van Williams, spoke from the perspective of 2011. "I'm not sure, that *King of Kings* didn't maybe hurt him some," Williams said. "Like *Green Hornet* hurt me, and *Batman* hurt Adam (West).

"He didn't get anything after that that was as big. That was a big budget movie, he was the major star, he was raved about, he did an excellent job, and it hurt him."[9]

Sam Bronston, the film's producer, bluntly said he thought the film disintegrated Hunter's career.[10]

Frontier Justice. *(Photofest)*

King of Kings was greeted with the usual mix of reaction upon its release, as some critics loved it and others did not. Some writers, especially those in the religious press, questioned the liberties the film had taken with Bible stories and whether Hunter had been the right choice for the role.

The film gave Hunter enormous visibility around the world, increasing his fan mail tremendously. Years later, he was still receiving thousands of letters a month.

"There are some things," Hunter said, "That can't be measured in dollars and sense."[11]

True enough. Still, it nagged that the film created almost no big screen career momentum. It hadn't given Hunter protection from the ups and downs of Hollywood. It was almost as if Hollywood film producers disregarded his contribution to the film.

The actor lost out on good roles in films such as *PT 109* and *The Caretakers* in the months following the release of *King of Kings* and there had been the usual assortment of film proposals that didn't materialize, as is common to all careers in Hollywood.

His was a solid, working class actor's career, the same as it had been since he had landed the role of Martin Pawley in *The Searchers* in 1955. He hadn't moved into the upper echelon of film stars, but the truth, then and now, was that few do.

By 1963, the question for Jeffrey Hunter had become: if there had been interesting roles in the past couple of years on television, why not give series television a try?

NBC liked the *Temple Houston* test film and targeted the series for a premiere no earlier than as a January 1964 midseason replacement, or, more likely, as a premiere for the fall 1964–65 season.

Hunter was new to a starring role in series television, but not to television work itself. In the 1950s, he had made a few guest appearances on network anthology programs, and more recently his appearances as a guest star on episodic television shows had taken on a different flavor, as he often traded in his nice guy image in feature films for more complicated character parts.

Hunter's guest shots on the *Bob Hope Presents the Chrysler Theatre* before and after *Temple Houston*'s production schedule typify the period. In 1963, he played a drifter falsely accused of murder in a small town in "Seven Miles of Bad Road," and his co-stars were Eleanor Parker and Neville Brand; in 1964, he played Barry Stinson, a parolee planning to rob the post office at a seminary in "Parties to the Crime"; his co-stars were Darren McGavin and Sally Kellerman.

"I love television," Hunter said. "It's just like making motion pictures except that the pace is faster. It means hard work, but the harder I work, the happier I am.

"In TV, every show presents a challenge and by being constantly on the job, as one in a series, you can't help but become a better actor."[12]

In March 1963, Jack Warner and the Warner Brothers Studio announced that Hunter had been signed to a long-term contract for both film and television work, and in June, Conrad directed Hunter and new co-star Jack Elam (replacing James Coburn, who had appeared in the March pilot) in a series of photographic test shots to get the ball rolling on a second *Temple Houston* pilot. Hunter's production company owned a piece of the show.

All appeared well. There was reason to believe that the new contract, the Ford film, and the primetime series would be a boost to Hunter's career.

It was while Hunter and his family were vacationing in Acapulco in July that things changed that summer of 1963. Jack Webb at Warner Brothers got in touch with an urgent message—NBC had suddenly pulled the plug on another series due to premiere that fall, *The Robert Taylor Show*, and *Temple Houston* was being rushed into production.

For series lead Jeffrey Hunter, there would be no time for the role in *The Long Flight* for John Ford, and there'd be precious little time to even prep the weekly show. It was due to premiere in September.

Longtime MGM star and box office champion Robert Taylor hadn't been planning on returning to a starring role in a television series in 1963. In fact, after his series *Robert Taylor's Detectives* finished its three year run in 1962, Taylor had been adamant: he was returning to films.

It wasn't that Taylor hadn't enjoyed working on *Detectives*, a police drama that had aired on both NBC and ABC during its run. In fact, he had enjoyed it quite a bit. But he wasn't ready for another series. "After several years of a weekly grind, you feel numb," he said. "Not that I was bored with my series. Actually, it was stimulating to work hard at a deadline pace, knowing no one will excuse even one day's delay."[13]

The Detectives had produced almost one hundred episodes in both hour long and half-hour-long form between 1959 and 1962. When it ended, Taylor's first film out of the gate was Disney's *Miracle of the White Stallions*, a 1963 drama about a colonel's attempts to protect stallions in the days of World War II Austria.

Jeffrey Hunter and co-star Jack Elam, August 1963. *(Photofest)*

"You must understand, going from this furious pace into the Disney picture, where we took plenty of time, was like a vacation for me," Taylor said.[14]

The film's release was a welcome return to the big screen for fan favorite Taylor, whose long and successful Hollywood career dated to 1934 at MGM and included films such as *Magnificent Obsession, Waterloo Bridge, Bataan,* and *Quo Vadis.*

"He was a dream to work with," Christopher Knopf, who'd written for *Robert Taylor's Detectives,* said. "Absolutely no problem whatsoever, a decent, respectful fellow."[15]

Taylor's MGM contracts had not permitted him to perform much on television, but when his last deal with MGM expired in 1958, he had turned to television, lured by the steady work and good paycheck when it appeared that his choice of films roles might not be what it had been in the past.

Television was the "next logical step" in the actor's career. "Movie parts for me weren't so easy to find anymore," Taylor said.[16] *Robert Taylor's Detectives* had been a commercial and critical success for the networks and its producing studio, Four Star Television.

Robert Taylor as Captain Matt Holbrook in *The Detectives Starring Robert Taylor,* aka *Robert Taylor's Detectives,* 1959.

The offer of a new television series with Four Star came to Taylor late in the fall 1962.

"I was determined to stay on the movie side," Taylor said. "But here's where the human element comes in.

"Four Star, in which I'm a stockholder, had this series based on the Department of Health, Education, and Welfare. I saw it as even a more provocative series than *The Detectives,* one with informational public service as well as dramatic excitement.

"And when I was told that NBC wouldn't buy this series unless I starred in it, that is where the human element comes in. The flattery was irresistible and besides, my stock in the company would go up a few points with another series sale."[17]

Taylor was cast as Christopher Logan, a special assistant to the Secretary of Health, Education, and Welfare. Logan would take on a wide range of assignments for HEW, opening up the story possibilities. While Logan was an expert in issues being tackled by Health, he also supervised activities of other agencies. The cases would involve issues such as epidemics, illegal adoptions, narcotics, civil defense, and illegal adoptions.

As the series was being developed, Taylor became genuinely excited by the high quality of the scripts he was seeing. "We have some wonderful writers who are making some dramatic pearls out of worthy themes," he said.[18]

The pilot, for example, was written by Bruce Geller, and was set in Los Angeles as a search was underway for a man who may have contracted a deadly plague. Bernard Kowalski directed; Robert Loggia was a co-star. True to form at Four Star in those days, the pilot was a high-quality, fast-moving, well-produced show.

"The series has got to be a smash," Taylor said.[19]

But the series never got a chance to be a smash or anything else. On July 17th, NBC abruptly cancelled it, despite the fact that several episodes had already been produced and a half dozen sponsors were lined up. Instead, the network said it was going with *Temple Houston*. The western series was put on the production schedule, aimed at a September airdate.

In making its decision in the manner that it did, NBC effectively sealed the fate of two television franchises. *The Robert Taylor Show* would never see the light of day, and, in the end, *Temple Houston* hardly stood a chance. NBC, Warner Brothers, and even Four Star would all end up in weaker positions as a result.

It is impossible to say what the fate of the two franchises would have been, had NBC stuck to its original plan, and kept the Taylor series on the air and given the Hunter series proper time to gear up. In television, one never knows, but it is possible—just possible—that both series would have enjoyed healthy runs on the network.

Instead, history happened another way.

Temple Houston has most often been dismissed as simply a failed one-season western drama on television. Fair enough—so it was. But the story of *Temple Houston* is more than that; it is also the story of the intersection points between careers, Hollywood studios, and network television.

The series is significant in that it was the first product out of Jack Webb's tenure at Warner Brothers; it also represents one of the first times Warner Brothers allowed an actor to have a financial stake in one of its television properties.

And certainly, *Temple Houston* was anything but a typical Warner Brothers series in that it was produced at such a breathtaking pace, breathtaking even by primetime television standards, necessitated by the late call from NBC.

From the beginning, *Temple Houston*, born of chaos, was chaos itself.

§

ENDNOTES
1. Smith, "Better Late Than Never for Webb," Sec. IV, page 12.
2. Windsor, interview.
3. Finnigan, "Actor Hunter to Have Eyes of Texas on Him," page 3-C.
4. Spiro, "TV Plum Eludes Robert Taylor," July 26, 1963
5. Fitzsimons, interview.
6. "Ten Push-Ups and I Simmer Down," page 28.
7. MacMinn, page D 2
8. Pruess, page 29
9. Williams, interview
10. "Big Picture- Maker Samuel Bronston Based in Dallas for Comeback Drive."
11. Grant, "Jeff Hunter Breaks Hollywood Jinx," page 7
12. Spiro, July 26, 1963
13. Grant, "Bob Taylor Back on TV with Exciting New Series," page 6 G
14. Ibid
15. Knopf, e-mail, January 17, 2011
16. Grant, "Bob Taylor Back on TV with Exciting New Series," page 6 G
17. Ibid
18. Ibid
19. Ibid

Chapter Two
Then Gallop

In the episode "Do Onto Others, Then Gallop," Temple Houston is lying on the bed in his cell, propped up on one arm, with a blanket over him, eating peanuts. He's been jailed as a suspect in the gunning down of an innocent man and hasn't had any luck in proving his innocence. The town has turned against Houston, too.

Into the jail comes Harmony, the man who put the whole con game into motion, for revenge's sake. Harmony reveals that his real name is Reed and that his father was Jeremy Reed, law partner to Temple's father, Sam Houston. The elder Reed was caught taking bribes and the elder Houston had him sent to jail.

Harmony has come to the jail to kill Houston because the con game is falling apart. Marshal Taggart has arrested some of those involved and is in the process of questioning them. Harmony knows it is only a matter of time before they talk and Houston is cleared.

Houston tells him that he's got a gun under the blanket and that it is pointed right at Harmony's stomach.

Harmony scoffs at what he believes to be a bluff and he reaches for his gun. From under the blanket comes the sound of a gun being cocked. Harmony's hand stops its reach.

Houston commands Harmony to turn his gun over, which he does. Only then does Houston reveal that there was no gun under the blanket—only a peanut shell. Houston pressed his thumb and index finger against the shell, mimicking the sound of a gun cocking.

The shell game, Houston says.[1]

Veteran television writer Ron Bishop, later to become even more well known for his literate scripts for *Gunsmoke*, used what he said was something that actually happened—the peanut shell trick—as a means to resolve the conflict in his story.[2] Bishop, a highly skilled writer of the television Western, built to the moment

Jeffrey Hunter as Temple Houston.
(Western TV Photos)

perfectly in his script; it was a clever and charming blend of Western history and fictional television narrative as seen by NBC audiences in 1964 as one of the last episodes of *Temple Houston*.

This is the kind of moment the creative team behind a television series hopes to offer, week after week. Weekly narrative television is about moments as much as anything else. This was the challenge to the people behind *Temple Houston*, who produced twenty-six episodes of television—the equivalent of thirteen feature films—between August 1963 and March 1964.

This is just one of the many "What ifs" in the history of the program. What if the series hadn't been rushed into production that summer, and the writers and producers had been given more time to develop their scripts as they had originally hoped? Would things have been different?

Jeffrey Hunter thought so. "Those shows in the end had humor. Action was built around town characters. We would build a sequence on them."[3]

"Do Onto Others, Then Gallop," was the kind of story Hunter and the producers had hoped to tell more of when work commenced on the original series pilot in March 1963, and then on the series itself. Hopes had been high. NBC had liked the pilot, and bought the series, making it the first success for Jack Webb at the helm of Warner Brothers Television. But the full story of the *Temple Houston* series goes back a little further than these events in the first quarter of 1963. The story actually began much earlier.

In the late 1950s, Warner Brothers was one of the chief program suppliers to ABC. Not all of the series had been successful, of course, but many had been—the list included series such as *Cheyenne*, *Sugarfoot*, and *Bronco*. The Western dominated television in these years, and Warner Brothers was producing several of the most popular examples of the genre. *Maverick*, starring James Garner, premiered in the fall of 1957 and stands today as a television classic.

As a matter of course, the studio was always looking for the next property. The studio, for example, had in its files a short biography on the life of Temple Houston by Glenn Shirley, as well as a story treatment on another real life figure, Moman Prueitt, who was also a well-known attorney in the American Southwest. Both ideas had been rejected and then filed away.[4]

In 1961, there was renewed discussion at Warner Brothers about doing a series on a frontier attorney. These rejected proposals were brought back out for reconsideration, and it was decided to develop a series around Temple Houston. Choosing between the two men was easy for studio writers James Barnett and Harry Fried, producer Richard Bluel and others at Warner Brothers developing the property: Temple Houston, Barnett said, was the more colorful of the two men, and had led a more adventurous life. Houston provided the unique combination of being clever and good with his guns. Prueitt, on the other hand, had spent his legal career, according to studio research, trying to free criminals who were guilty.

Besides, Barnett wrote, Temple Houston was the name for a hero.[5]

Hunter enjoyed his role as Temple Houston.
(Western TV Photos)

Temple Lea Houston was part of one of the most famous families in Texas history, and he left his own mark, as well. Born August 12, 1860, the last child of Sam Houston and the first child born in the governor's mansion in Austin. Houston's father died when he was three. He worked as a page for the U.S. Senate in Washington, D.C., studying law, and returned to Texas and attended Texas A&M and Baylor University Law School. In 1881, he was appointed district attorney in the Texas Panhandle. As Lee Phillips wrote, "He soon acquired a reputation as a ferocious, eloquent and picturesque lawyer, customarily dressing in buckskins with Old Betsy strapped to his waist." [6]

Houston's life was nothing if not colorful. He was a brilliant trial attorney, and renowned for his speeches in court. He often dressed flamboyantly, wearing a beaded vest and rattlesnake tie. He gave the dedication address for the opening of the Texas capital in 1888, and served as a state senator, before moving to Woodward, Oklahoma in 1894.

He moved to Oklahoma because he was determined to carve his own history, and escape the shadow of his famous father. Eventually, he became involved in the fight for Oklahoma statehood.

To this day, Houston is remembered for his 1899 "Soiled Dove Plea" in Woodward on behalf of his client, a prostitute. The closing argument is studied as a supremely delivered speech in a court of law. In it Houston urged the all-male jury to "judge her gently," and the accused was set free.

Like many larger-than-life figures from Western history, Houston's life has its share of tall tales. It was often said, for example, that in his life Houston crossed paths with Billy the Kid and Bat Masterson, and once bested The Kid in a shooting match that Masterson arranged. As historian Glenn Shirley pointed out, by the time Houston got to Tascosa, Masterson was gone and Billy the Kid had been dead ten months.[7]

But Tascosa was one of the wildest towns in the West, and as Shirley wrote, "Temple did, however, enthusiastically inject himself into the pageantry that kept the town in a constant state of expectancy."[8]

It is true, however, that Houston was involved in a shoot-out in Oklahoma in 1895, in which Ed Jennings, a lawyer, was killed. The case went to trial in 1896, and a coroner ruled that Jennings was killed by a shot in the back of the head, likely from his own brother.

Temple Houston died early, at the age of 45, felled by a cerebral hemorrhage, but he left his mark on history. As noted by biographer Glenn Shirley, "…he lived far beyond his years, realized the ambitions of his profession before reaching his majority, and drained the cup of life. For more than two decades, from 1881 to 1905, he was one of the Southwest's most brilliant, eccentric, and widely known criminal lawyers.

"One journalist has capsulized him as a 'gun-toting, tough hombre and silver-tongued darling of the frontier courtroom—a very dangerous man to oppose in a lawsuit; he could beat any man making a speech I ever heard talk'..."[9]

Needless to say, these and other stories from Houston's life made him an attractive target for Hollywood. In 1961, Warner Brothers approached the idea again as some of its other Western series on ABC-TV began to run out of steam.

James Barnett of Warner Brothers wrote a five-page treatment for the series, dated September 1961, based on research the studio had previously collected. While there were fictionalized characters in this proposal, Houston himself was being presented, as Barnett said himself, fairly factually. But that didn't last very long.

Barnett's original proposal said that the show was meant to stride alongside history in the making because Temple Houston had made history. The proposal said the series would not be a slick, facile show but would be based in the harsh truth

Hunter as the real-life Temple Houston.
(Western TV Photos)

of the times in which Houston lived. The proposal said the stories would be based in fact, not fiction, because Houston's life was full of dramatic possibilities. Houston would be portrayed as he actually was, in those years at the close of the 19th Century.[10]

After further discussion, it was decided that more liberties would be taken with the character and the series premise, and in early 1962 a new series proposal was drafted, adding new characters, subtracting others, and making Houston a defense attorney instead of a prosecutor, as he was in real life.[11]

Among the recurring characters were a deputy marshal who would be a friend and foil to Temple Houston, and a judge for the circuit court with which Houston rode.

There was also a great deal of attention paid to the law as it was in Houston's time, and the struggle to establish a true system of law and order. It was thought that many actual frontier truths would add to the color of the stories individually and therefore to the series as a whole: the idea that everyone, including lawyers and judges, wore their guns to court, for example; the colorful language and ideas expressed by those with and without a formal education, legal or otherwise; the idea of the roving court and the wild atmosphere surrounding its arrival in communities where the court was for many the only real entertainment; and the real life legal cases, so different from the issues explored in more modern times.[12]

It was decided to base the first script on an existing Warner Brothers property, "Galahad of Cactus Spring," a story by the prolific film writer Philip Lonergan that had been kicking around one Hollywood studio or another since the era of silent films, Lonergan's heyday. His story about a frontier attorney was used as the basis for the story.[13] This was common practice for the studio in those days—using an existing studio property as the basis for a project to maintain ownership and avoid the "created by" credits.[14]

Purposefully, Barnett and others working on the series format and the first script had moved the show away from a truly factual portrayal of the real-life Temple Houston, with the exception of the use of his name, the fact that he was the son of Sam Houston, and the use of Texas as the locale. From this development schedule in 1961 and 1962 came the script for what be the original test film for *Temple Houston*, starring Jeffrey Hunter, which was shot in March 1963.

This test film from Warner Brothers would be at least the fourth time that Houston's life had, in one way or another, formed the basis for a product of mass media. The dramatic possibilities of Houston's life had been recognized before; the studio's challenge was to distinguish their effort from what had come before, including other television westerns of the time and other media works based on Houston's life.

In 1960, an independent film titled *Oklahoma Territory* was released, starring actor Bill Williams as Temple Houston. The 67-minute film depicted the story of the efforts to solve the murder of a local Indian agent.

Novelist Edna Ferber, famous for *Cimarron*, had based the character of Yancy Cravat on Temple Houston in her work, which was filmed twice, once in 1930 starring Richard Dix and then again in 1960 starring Glenn Ford.

Ferber's actions had not gone over well with Houston's descendants, who felt she had misled them about her intentions. The family said it had been under the impression that she was writing a factual book about Temple Houston, not using the events of his life to write a "hay-loft" novel.[15]

As the series format was being developed, Warner Brothers sent a letter to the postmaster at Woodward, asking if any direct descendants of Temple Houston were still alive and living there.[16] As it turned out, two of Houston's children were still alive, and Bessie Houston, wife of Temple Houston's son Richard, sent a letter to the studio, dated February 26, 1962, saying, "We are very much interested in anything concerning Temple Houston and especially writings about his life..."[17]

"Mainly we were interested in seeing the film company's material and tracing the source of the material," Richard Houston said. "We didn't want my father's memory distorted. The film company's attorney wrote back that they had all the information they wished on Temple Houston, and that my father was a 'public character' and could be presented as they saw fit."[18]

Temple Houston's widow had won a libel suit in the 1920s against *Liberty* magazine, which had described Temple Houston as an outlaw and that his mother was a Cherokee Indian, neither of which was true.

Richard Houston told *The Dallas Morning News*, "We would have been proud if my grandmother had been an Indian. We just wanted to get the facts straight. We still do."[19]

Internal memos from Warner Brothers reveal that the studio went back and forth on the issue of whether or not to use the name of Temple Houston, or use another name entirely; one memo suggesting changing the name of the character made sense because the character bore no resemblance to the real person, anyway.[20]

There were concerns about the legal issues involved, concerns about how living relatives might react, and at one time it was suggested that perhaps the studio should simply reach a settlement with Houston's two living heirs before heading into production.[21]

An inter-office communication at Warner Brothers, dated April 19, 1962, said that as long as the studio portrayed all deceased actual persons accurately or more favorably than they were in real life, that the risk of a liability was small.[22]

As late as March 1963, as the first pilot was going into production, the idea of adding a disclaimer to the pilot and the series, to the effect that the stories were suggested by the life of Temple Houston, but were fictionalized, was being seriously considered.[23]

In the end, attorneys decided that there was no legal objection to the series, because, they said, the show was based on historical facts and fictionalized events, did not portray any living persons, and Houston was portrayed in what was essentially a favorable light.

In describing the family's feelings about the series, author Bernice Tune wrote that the television series "did much damage to the brilliant man's memory...he was portrayed as an itinerate gun-slinging lawyer with a glib tongue...it failed in that in displaying his characteristics of being innately gentle, non-conformist, the soul of wanderlust, trustful and honest, it came out that he was flagrant in his use of the law and went out in search of clients. This he never had to do. His popularity was such that he practiced at the beck and call of the people of four states."[24]

Family and friends, according to Tune, did agree that Jeffrey Hunter had a slight resemblance to the real Temple Houston.[25]

While episodes of the series do not depict events in Houston's life in the history book sense, several do take facts and incidents from that time period—the use of a 'hanging' judge in "Gallows at Galilee" for instance—and build stories around them. Houston is clearly the central character and the hero of the series and is portrayed as such.

Bringing justice to the frontier.
(*Western TV Photos*)

In response to a letter from James Wong, the manager of the Woodward, Oklahoma Chamber of Commerce, Jack Webb said the studio's hope for the series was to be entertaining, not to present a historically accurate look at the times.[26]

By the time Webb wrote that response, in April 1963, the pilot had been shot. The fact that the pilot had taken almost two years to reach fruition was nothing new in Hollywood. Webb's interest had done a lot to make the pilot a reality.

Webb was hired in February 1963, as the executive in charge of television production at the studio; Jack Warner called it the first step toward retooling the television division. Warner's goal was to make the studio a leader once again in television film production. For several years Warner Brothers had enjoyed an exclusive contract with ABC, filling several hours of the primetime schedule.

However, the studio's share of primetime real estate had started to slip dramatically in the previous year. In 1962, Warner Brothers could claim eight hours of airtime, but for the fall of 1963, it had only series, *77 Sunset Strip*, on the schedule of any network, and it was facing cancellation.

Webb's task was to get Warner Brothers back to the top of the heap. That meant keeping *77 Sunset Strip* on the schedule and selling new series for air sometime in 1964, be it a midseason addition, or be it for the full 1964–65 season.[27]

Webb's career in radio and television had well prepared him for this moment. He was a prolific actor, writer, producer, and director of franchises in radio, television, and film, most prominently, of course, *Dragnet*, the police drama that would prove to be the godfather of all police dramas to follow in television. Webb was just coming off a cancelled series, *GE True*, which he produced independently, when Jack Warner reached out with the orders to add some energy to the studio television product.

Webb had some definite ideas how to do so. He told reporters that he was tired of morose stories, that he remembered the time, years before, when Warner Brothers was the first major studio to move into television. Webb said he appreciated the studio's history of turning out "nice, clean stories, about nice, clean people at a time when audiences were getting tired of the whole scratching, mumbling, torn undershirt kind of thing."

Webb managed to keep *77 Sunset Strip* on the air by completely revamping the program, changing its format radically, and opening the 1963 season with a five part episode.

The new executive also studied the list of television projects at Warner Brothers, and just a few weeks into his tenure he held a press conference to detail what was seen as a vigorous program to re-establish Warner Brothers as a force to be reckoned with in television, using what Webb called a "new concept in television production."

Webb announced that the studio's exclusive contract with ABC was a thing of the past, believing it was better to deal with all three networks. Webb also said that the studio would sign actors and independent producers to participation deals, a major change from previous studio policy. Webb said that sharing series ownership would attract stars to television.[28]

Bette Davis signed a co-production deal to star in a dramatic series about an interior decorator; George Burns signed to co-produce a comedy series; and Jeffrey Hunter signed a deal to co-produce and star in the western series *Temple Houston*. Webb also announced deals for a series starring Dorothy Provine, a series based on the hit play and film *No Time for Sergeants*, a drama called *The Federal Investigators*, and a series based on John Steinbeck's *Travels with Charley*.

Of these proposals, *Temple Houston*, *Wendy and Me* from George Burns, and *No Time for Sergeants* would make it to air as a series. Though none would be ratings hits, and the *77 Sunset Strip* gamble would result in the cancellation of the former hit series in early 1964, Webb's batting average, at least in terms of getting pilots on as a series, wasn't bad and could have been worse.

Temple Houston became the first Warner series to air on a network other than ABC when it was purchased by NBC.

Webb's tenure as head of television at Warner Brothers was, however, brief; Jack Warner, who had signed Webb to a guaranteed, $150,000 a year, three year deal, fired him that December. Webb had told Warner when he was hired that the job to turn around the studio's television fortunes would take two to three years, but Warner was impatient, and rehired the man Webb had replaced, William T. Orr.[29]

However, it is important to keep in mind that for whatever problems that may or may not have been associated with Webb's stay at Warner Brothers, he did pull off a miracle of television production—getting *Temple Houston* to air on time in September, after the late call from NBC in July. As author Michael J. Hayde described it, "it was a profound example of swift professionalism."[30] Indeed, Webb threw the whole show together in a matter of days that summer.

But back to March and April first.

Production on the pilot was scheduled for filming in March, and given a nine-day shooting schedule—not unheard for long form pilots in those days.

Hunter's contract for the test film, dated March 7, 1963, was for the sum of $5,000 for eight days, and $1,000 a day for each additional day's work. Interim payments at a rate of $1,250 a week would begin just after the pilot was completed and continue for twelve weeks, or until the series was picked up, or until the studio hired Hunter for work in a feature film, whichever came first. Hunter's series option, during which time the studio could engage his services in the role of Temple Houston, extended until April 1, 1964.

That first contract also made provisions for the payment schedules that would result should the series be picked up, including the starting per-episode rate of $5,000; $500 for reruns up to the sixth run of each episode; and payment for any theatrical exhibition of series episodes anywhere in the world at the rate of $5,000 per episode. Additional compensation for the sale of the series overseas was included in the contract; Hunter would receive $500 for each run of an episode, up to six runs, whenever an episode was released on television in any city in the world.[31]

Temple Houston was sold to NTV of Japan even before its premiere in the United States; it premiered in the United Kingdom in October 1964, and ran in Australia starting in 1966.

Hunter's $5,000 per episode pay scale for the series was typical of the going rate for series leads in those days, assuming a seven day shoot, with overtime pay of about $500 a day. Projected over a season of 26 episodes, the deal was good for about $130,000 a year.

The series resulting from the successful sale of the pilot would be produced by a joint venture between Warner Brothers (80%) and Hunter's Apollo Productions (20%).[32]

The joint venture between Warners and Hunter to produce the series came to be called The Temple Houston Company.

While the idea of giving stars a piece of the show was new to the studio, it was not all that new to Hunter's career. He had formed a production company before, and had a hand in the production of the 1955 documentary short *The Living Swamp* and the 1959 documentary *La cuidad Sagrada*.

The film end of the contract guaranteed Hunter work in a picture budgeted at not less than $750,000 each year the series was on the air. The pay scale on the films was targeted as follows: $75,000 for the film produced during the first season, $100,000 for the second, $125,000 for the third, $150,000 for the fourth, and $200,000 for the fifth year of the show (by way of comparison, Hunter had been paid $50,000 for his work a few years earlier in *Sergeant Rutledge*,[33] also produced by Warner Brothers, and received $100,000 for *King of Kings*).[34]

The test film, with on-screen writing credits shared by Dean Reisner and Michael Zagor, told the story of how Temple Houston came to Tascosa, Texas as part of the circuit court, and became involved with an old flame and her husband, who has been charged with murder. A former business associate was blackmailing Houston's old flame and the blackmailer is subsequently killed. Houston must employ all sorts of courtroom tactics to get his clients off. Along the way, he cons the circuit court judge and picks up all kinds of clients.

The script drew from the concept put forward in the series proposal, which described Tascosa as a wild town where law and order was hard to maintain, a place where court week was almost like the carnival coming to town.

People came in from all over to watch justice being done in the makeshift courtroom; horse races and spelling bees were among the events held to entertain the crowds.[35]

Reisner and Zagor's script opened with a parade in Tascosa, held to welcome the circuit court to town. A band plays, and the members of the court are cheered like celebrities or conquering heroes. Houston tips his hat and yells 'howdy' to the crowd, and it is clear from the first moments of the pilot that this was intended to be a different kind of western.

Temple Houston would not only combine of two popular television genres, the western and the legal drama, but it would do so with a sense of humor. Houston himself was portrayed as a flamboyant, brilliant, and charming man.

"We know that he grew up to be quite a character," Hunter said. "He wore his hair long and flowing like Buffalo Bill.

"I'll admit I don't look like the real Temple Houston in the least in my role. How do you think TV watchers would accept a young western hero with long, flowing hair?"[36]

Hunter was costumed in black pants, knee-high boots, a ruffled shirt, and a string tie. From scene to scene in the pilot, Hunter is relaxed and clearly relishing the part.

"I like the premise of this show and the character I'm playing," Hunter said. "It's pure entertainment as opposed to the personal problems as dramatized in medical and psycho-medical programs. There's nothing wrong with those shows, I'm just contrasting them with what we're doing.

"We can have a lot of fun with this thing. I've been reading transcripts of his courtroom oratory and it was flamboyant. He was clever with a jury, playing on their emotion."[37]

As laid out in the series proposal, Houston had a sidekick, Tod Grey, whom he called 'Stonewall.' Played by Martin Best, Grey was an attorney in training who was seen in the pilot to not only run Houston's errands but also to do some of his legal research, such as contacting the Pinkerton detectives to discover what background information might be available on a witness who could be potentially damaging to Houston's client. Tod Grey idolized Temple Houston and wanted to follow in his footsteps.

(Another office assistant was originally envisioned for the series, but was among those characters dropped as the development of the series format progressed. Beaumont Tillinghast had been described as an elderly, balding man; he was Houston's records keeper, and a man who could hold his liquor and handle a gun.)[38]

Rounding out the cast were James Coburn as Boyd Palmer, a deputy U.S. marshal skeptical of Houston; Preston Foster as a good times loving judge; Joanna Moore as Houston's old flame, Kevin Hagen as her husband; Ed Nelson as Marteen, the blackmailer; and Sherwood Price as George Taggart, the potentially damaging witness against Houston's clients.

The casting was one of the strong points of the pilot. When the pilot eventually was released theatrically, *Variety* said, "Hunter is colorful as the cocky lawyer, Preston Foster correctly irritable as a circuit judge, James Coburn reliable as a rather hapless marshal, Joanna Moore pretty and sincere as the accused woman."[39]

Jack Webb executive produced the pilot, which was filmed between March 12th and March 21st, and ran about 57 minutes. Michael Meshekoff, who started with Webb on the *Dragnet* days in radio and television, produced the film, and William Conrad ably directed. Conrad, superb as Marshal Matt Dillon in *Gunsmoke* on CBS radio for nine years, had developed into a very capable director, and his shot sequences kept the first *Temple Houston* story moving along at an enjoyable pace.

The *Temple Houston* pilot was everything Jack Warner had been hoping for when he brought Webb on to turn things around at Warner Brothers Television—slick, well-produced, and successful. NBC liked the program and bought it, aiming for an airdate sometime in 1964, either as a midseason replacement in January or as a new program in September.

The successful production of the pilot was quickly followed by an official announcement by Jack Warner that Warner Brothers had signed Hunter to the long-term contract. Hunter would star in the series and headline a film a year for the studio for as long as the series ran.[40]

For Jeffrey Hunter, the contract with Warner Brothers would mean security and guaranteed work, if the series proved to be a success.

The wheels were turning at Warner Brothers in terms of how to capitalize on its new star, and projected new series.

The decision had been made to discard the first pilot as fare for the series. Instead, an additional thirty minutes of footage would be shot, added onto the original test film, and it would be released overseas as a feature film. This studio hoped this would serve to further promote the series, as well as grease the wheels a little bit for what the studio hoped would be a successful overseas syndication deal for the series.

Next, the studio and the network decided to shoot a second pilot, 60 minutes in length, perhaps in color, with financing by NBC, for airing on the network.[41]

James Coburn didn't want anything to do with a regular role in a television series, and backed out of the project. His option had passed, and nothing Webb could say to him would convince him to change his mind, but that was a problem only for the series domestically. The first pilot would be shown only overseas, anyway, and the new footage needed to pad the length could heavily feature Jeff Hunter.[42]

Fortunately for the *Temple Houston* production, another Warner Brothers series, *The Dakotas*, had been cancelled, leaving character actor Jack Elam available. He was quickly connected to the *Houston* project as Houston's foil, or as Elam described it, as "Hunter's Devil."[43] The marshal was meant to serve at times as Houston's antagonist, and at others as his ally. The character was named George Taggart, but was not the same character as the Taggart depicted in the pilot.

In June, Hunter was called to the studio for what was the start of the 'second pilot' for *Temple Houston*; William Conrad directed a series of photographic test shots of Hunter and his new co-star, using part of the draft script for the second pilot being written by James Warner Bellah, the historian-novelist-screen writer.

Bellah's involvement with the project was considered a coup for the project. Bellah had written stories that served as the basis for some of John Ford's most successful Westerns, including *Fort Apache*, *She Wore a Yellow Ribbon*, and *Rio Grande*. He had co-authored the screenplay for *Sergeant Rutledge*, directed by Ford and starring Jeff Hunter, and *The Man Who Shot Liberty Valance*, released the previous year.

Bellah was not unfamiliar with the television format, having written the script for a produced, though unsold, pilot, based on the cavalry and the character of Nathan Brittles, the one played by John Wayne in *She Wore a Yellow Ribbon*. The half-hour show did air on the anthology series *The Best of the Post* in 1960.

Bellah's draft script for *Temple Houston* was based on his story line and treatment, which had already been approved by NBC.

It was NBC's intention that Bellah deliver the final draft of his script no later than July 11th. NBC would then decide whether to order the production and delivery of the one-hour pilot. If NBC took the option by July 18th, the finished pilot would be due by September 1st.[44]

Bellah delivered his script in plenty of time; the murder mystery was an ambitious attempt to stake the series as a high-quality production.

NBC had creative approval over the producer, director, and all major casting of the second pilot, which was budgeted up to $167,500.[45]

Hunter had signed a new contract with the studio on June 20th, replacing the deal he had signed in March. This contract would pay him $7,000 for eight days on the second pilot, $1,000 for each additional day's work beyond eight days, and extended the network's series option until May 4, 1964. Further, the new contract obligated the studio to engage Hunter in a feature theatrical motion picture at $75,000 for ten

Jack Elam as Deputy Marshal George Taggart. (*Western TV Photos*)

weeks; this picture would be in addition to the other contracted theatrical picture commitment of one film each year of the television series contract.

The theatrical pictures portion of the deal was job security for Hunter. Each picture would be budgeted at no less than $750,000, and his per-picture salary would climb over the five-year deal from $75,000 to $200,000, a jump of $25,000 a year. Additionally, Warner Bros. agreed to pay him 50% of the salary if the studio did not exercise the picture option in any given year.[46]

The announcement on the first motion picture assignment came from Jack Warner in early July. Hunter would be the fifth star to join the eight-star cast of John Ford's *The Long Flight*. [47]

The casting of Hunter made sense for any number of reasons—Hunter was an old-hand on Ford films, having made three with the famous director (*The Searchers*, *The Last Hurrah*, and *Sergeant Rutledge*); Hunter was happy to work with Ford again; Ford was gathering many of his long-time crew members and actors together for one last Western; and it would benefit the studio and the new television series to once again showcase Hunter in a new film by Ford.

Hunter's connection with Ford went deeper than his appearances in the three films. Ford had also tried to cast Hunter in a fourth film, 1959's *The Horse Soldiers*, and it was Ford who had recommended Hunter for the role of Jesus in the 1961 epic *King of Kings*.

Hunter always did good work for the director. "Ford got performances out of people like Jeff Hunter," director Alvin Ganzer, who would direct for the *Temple Houston* series, said.[48]

The part in *The Long Flight* probably wouldn't have been much, really; Richard Widmark was the star of the picture. But that seemed almost beside the point to Hunter and everyone else taking parts in the film. It was Ford, a western, and back to Monument Valley one last time with one of the great American directors.

Undoubtedly, Hunter's screen time in the Ford film would also have benefitted *Temple Houston*, as a cross-promotion if nothing else, and if the series was still on the air. Further, co-star Jack Elam was cast in the Warners film *A Distant Trumpet*, a cavalry picture. Elam would receive extra exposure from that film, exposure that, once again, could only help the series.

Who knows? Maybe Ford could have been talked into directing an episode of *Temple Houston*. He'd done the same for Ward Bond on *Wagon Train* in 1960. There were a lot of possibilities on the horizon.

It seemed like the table was set. Hunter would first perform the lead in the second *Temple Houston* pilot film, then his role in *The Long Flight*, and then it would be on to the weekly series itself, to air some time in 1964. In the meantime, Hunter, Webb, and the studio could prep the series and get the scripts ready. All of these plans were laid out with the best of intentions that June and July. Everything was in place.

But that's when the roof fell in, and the gallop began.

§

ENDNOTES

1. "Do Unto Others, Then Gallop," written by Ron Bishop, Warner Bros. Archive, University of Southern California, Los Angeles.

2. Ibid, page 71

3. Pruess, page 29

4. Jim Barnett memo to Bryan Moore, March 14, 1963, Warner Bros. Archive, University of Southern California, Los Angeles.

5. Jim Barnett memo to Harry Fried, August 17, 1961, Warner Bros. Archive, University of Southern California, Los Angeles.

6. Phillips, page 24

7. Shirley, page 76.

8. Ibid

9. Shirley, page ix

10. *Temple Houston,* A one-hour filmed television presentation, September 11, 1961, Warner Bros. Archives, University of Southern California, Los Angeles.

11. Barnett to Moore memo, March 14, 1963

12. "Temple Houston and the Rise of Western Justice," *Temple Houston* format, July 5, 1962, Warner Bros. Archive, University of Southern California, Los Angeles.

13. Barnett to Moore memo, February 6, 1962, Warner Bros. Archive, University of Southern California, Los Angeles.

14. Anderson, page 276, as one example.

15. Tolbert, sec 1, page 24.

16. Carl Milliken letter to Postmaster, Woodward, Oklahoma, Warner Bros. Archive, University of Southern California, Los Angeles.

17. Bessie R. Houston letter to Carl Milliken, February 26, 1962, Warner Bros. Arhive, University of Southern California, Los Angeles.

18. Tolbert, sec 1, page 24.

19. Ibid.

20. Barnett memo to William T. Orr, February 27, 1962, Warner Bros. Archives, University of Southern California, Los Angeles.

21. Barnett memo to Orr, March 1, 1962, Warner Bros. Archives, University of Southern California, Los Angeles.

22. Bryan Moore memo to James Barnett, April 19, 1962, Warner Bros. Archives, University of Southern California, Los Angeles.

23. Bryan Moore memo to Michael Meshekoff, March 13, 1963, Warner Bros. Archive, University of Southern California, Los Angeles.

24. Tune, page 80

25. Ibid

26. Webb letter to James Wong, April 4, 1963, Warner Bros. Archives, University of Southern California, Los Angeles.

27. Anderson, pages 284- 286.

28. Smith, Cecil. "Jack Webb Tells Plans for 5 New TV Shows," page A 2

29. Anderson, page 286

30. Hayde, page 163.

31. Letter agreement between Jeffrey Hunter and Warner Bros. Pictures, March 7, 1963, Warner Bros. Archive, University of Southern California, Los Angeles.

32. Ibid

33. R.J. Obringer memo to Hal Holman, June 29, 1959, Warner Bros. Archive, University of Southern California, Los Angeles.

34. "Sheila Graham's Hollywood," *The Edmonton Journal,* page 29.

35. *Temple Houston,* A one-hour filmed television presentation, September 11, 1961, Warner Bros. Archives, University of Southern California, Los Angeles.

36. "Jeffrey Hunter Unlike Real-Life Temple Houston," sec. 4, page 4.

37. Finnigan, "Actor Hunter to Have Eyes of Texas on Him," page 3- C.

38. *Temple Houston,* A one-hour filmed television presentation, September 11, 1961, Warner Bros. Archives, University of Southern California, Los Angeles.

39. *The Man from Galveston, Variety,* January 15, 1964.

40. "Sign Hunter to Contract," page 13.

41. TV Teletype, page 6.

42. *Western Clippings,* page 8.

43. Finnigan, "Ex-Heavy Jack Elam Most Unusual Marshal," page 7 G

44. Sam Boverman letter to Bryan Moore, June 27, 1963, Warner Bros. Archives, The University of Southern California, Los Angeles.

45. Ibid

46. Letter agreement between Jeffrey Hunter and Warner Bros. Pictures, June 20, 1963, Warner Bros. Archive, University of Southern California, Los Angeles.

47. "Jeffrey Hunter in 'Flight,'" *The Hollywood Reporter*, July 15, 1963.

48. Ganzer, interview.

Chapter Three
Round the Clock at Warner Bros.

When it gave *Temple Houston* the green light, NBC was perfectly within its rights. The network was simply exercising its option under the contract signed with Warner Brothers. Its series option ran until 1964.

In business terms, NBC simply cancelled one series it was no longer interested in, *The Robert Taylor Show,* and replaced it with another property it was interested in, *Temple Houston.*

NBC replaced the Taylor series with *Temple Houston* because, the network said, the Hunter series was the one on hand that was furthest along in development and could be ready in time for the start of the fall season.

In practical terms, the impact on everyone was immediate. Hunter, for example, would not now be able to participate in *The Long Flight* (*Cheyenne Autumn*) with John Ford, and Jack Elam would not be able to take part in *A Distant Trumpet.* The production schedules collided.

Hunter's series deal called for him to be paid $7,000 for the first episode, as it was essentially the series second pilot, and $1,500 through Apollo Productions. His pay for subsequent episodes was $5,000 per and the $1,500 through Apollo Productions. If the series ran for five years, Hunter's pay would increase to as much as $6,600 per episode. Hunter was guaranteed thirteen episodes that first season.[1]

Jack Webb quickly shelved all plans to shoot additional footage to expand the original pilot, as well as all plans for a second, stand-alone, pilot.

All efforts had to go into getting *Temple Houston* to air on September 19th. August 7th was the projected date for film to roll. The first episode would essentially be the second pilot.

To say the cast and crew of *Temple Houston* were up against it does not come close to describing the challenge in front of them.

The stars of *Temple Houston*. (Western TV Photos)

The "furthest along" description used by NBC may have technically been the case, as compared to other potential series, but that doesn't mean *Temple Houston* was anywhere near ready for air. When the order came from NBC, nothing usable, in terms of being able to put together a complete episode, was on film.

The test shots done by Bill Conrad in June with Hunter and James Coburn's replacement, Jack Elam, were just that—test shots. No complete story lay underneath them.

Nor would the original pilot be used as the series' first episode, buying everyone some much needed time. The reason for keeping the original pilot on the shelf didn't have much to do, in the end, with continuity issues, although undoubtedly there were reasonable concerns about that. The sight of James Coburn as the marshal, for example, or Preston Foster as the judge, characters seen in the pilot but not destined for the series, might have been a little off-putting in terms of pure series continuity. However, their appearances could have easily been explained away in the second episode. Also, some editing could have been done quickly and easily to trim the pilot for time (somewhere between seven and nine minutes would have needed to have been cut). If required for exposition, an additional scene or two could have been shot; indeed, many television continuity issues could be handled easily with a simple voice-over narration.

For that matter, it was possible that the pilot, or parts of it, could be used as a series of flashback sequences in a new episode, which would serve to easily explain the appearance of Marshal Boyd Palmer and Judge Stark, characters which for one reason or another had been discarded.

None of these issues really stood in the way. A larger potential issue was that NBC had requested a format change.

"A series of circumstances changed the whole concept of the show dangerously," Hunter said later. "It was conceived in humor and delivered in dead seriousness."[2]

What the producers had tried for, and to some extent achieved, in the first test film, was a mix of drama and humor not unlike *Maverick*, but including *Perry Mason* style courtroom proceedings. There was more drama than in a typical *Maverick* episode, though, marking the series, in television descriptive terms, as a cross between *Maverick*, *Cheyenne*, and *Perry Mason*.

It was understood by those who made the pilot film that the Western had in many ways been played out on television by 1963; hundreds and hundreds of episodes in series after series had been produced by then. Westerns on television had utilized innumerable characters, settings, plots, and themes by 1963. Big stars had been featured in their own series. No-name stars had been given their own shows. Marshals, sheriffs, outlaws, widows, range wars, lynch mobs—you name it, and television westerns had done it. Ratings were down for many long-time hits, and some were ending their runs.

Something different was what was needed, like a lawyer on horseback, with humor. Pure entertainment, as Hunter called it. That was the idea.

NBC asked for a more serious tone to the series. *(Western TV Photos)*

However, NBC, in commissioning the series, asked for changes from the tone established in the pilot. The network was looking for was a much more straightforward western.

"When I said I'd do it," Hunter said. "There was a foundation of humor to the show. There was action, suspense, girls. But suddenly the network wanted a serious show."[3]

Perhaps the move to a more serious Western series was more in keeping with the tenor of the times, in the network's view. Many dramas in the early 1960s were steeped in the Kennedy New Frontier era of social realism. As the cowboy and the rancher left the television landscape, other, more urban professions, such as doctors, lawyers, and psychiatrists, were replacing them. Eighteen new dramas premiered in the fall of 1963, including *Channing* (college teacher), *East Side, West Side* (social worker), *Breaking Point* (psychiatrist), *The Greatest Show on Earth* (circus manager), and *Arrest and Trial* (lawyers and police investigators).

On NBC in particular, new series included *Mr. Novak*, about a public school teacher, *Redigo*, about a modern rancher, and *The Richard Boone Show*, an anthology. NBC was only introducing two new comedies into its fall lineup, *Grindl* and *Harry's Girls*.

But whatever reason was behind the network request to change the format, change it would. While the pilot could probably have been used, with some changes, it was decided that it would not be a part of the series. This decision added even more pressure onto a studio really scrambling to meet its airdate.

All the producers had on hand at the moment the series was optioned was three scripts in various stages of development, including the final draft script for the second pilot, titled "Two Murders at Noon," dated July 5, 1963. The pilot teleplay, written by James Warner Bellah, essentially served as the blueprint for the change in tone for series. The teleplay wasn't perfect—like most scripts, it needed work— but it did set the bar high in terms of how the series would be produced, and the relationship between Houston and Taggart.

"Two Murders at Noon" told the story of Temple Houston and George Taggart's involvement in solving two murders in the town of Brazoria. Three brothers have been accused of the crime but maintained their innocence. Houston takes on the job of their defense, while Taggart signs on as temporary deputy marshal to help arrest the brothers and maintain civil order as the trial approaches. Houston's investigation eventually reveals the brothers' sister, Dorrie, as the real killer.

The script had a large cast, with twenty-three characters with speaking parts, including Houston and Taggart, and plenty of extras needed to serve as townspeople, including jurors, spectators in the courtroom, bellhops, and judges' wives.

The set list of exteriors was extensive, including Main Street and the town square in Brazoria, the Cattlemen's National Bank, Noonan's Restaurant, a general store, the court house, the harness and undertaking, the sheriff's office, the U.S. marshal's office, the hotel, the boarding house, a local ranch, the trail outside of town, flatland near town, a rock formation, and so on.

Interior sets included the bank, the sheriff's office, the U.S. marshal's office, the hotel, the restaurant, the cellblock, the courtroom, and the hallway outside the courtroom.[4]

The most striking difference between the scripts for the first and second pilots was in the tone and overall approach, as requested by the network. While the first pilot had reflected the carnival atmosphere of the traveling court and the festive air it created in the towns it heard cases in, the script for the second pilot reflected a dirty, dusty and weary life in the American West.

When Temple Houston is first seen in "Two Murders at Noon," he is riding slowly and tiredly on the trail leading into Brazoria. He is filthy from the ride, exhausted, hungry, and in need of a shave. His clothes are worn out and so are his chaps. Reading these pages of Bellah's script is like reading one of his short stories; it's a page out of the old west.

This is also true when the audience is introduced to George Taggart, a page later. Taggart is as filthy as Houston.

As Bellah makes clear, the two characters have a history together—Taggart spent a year in jail for shooting a suspect in a murder case, and Houston prosecuted him. When they meet up on the trail outside of Brazoria in "Two Murders at Noon," they engage in a lengthy and savage fight, wary and untrusting of each other, although we see the bond of respect begin to build between them.

Eventually, the two men work together to help solve the murder mystery of the story, and Taggart agrees to ride along with Houston to the next town, to see how the lawyer makes out.

The script included Houston investigating the crime, and a court scene, and featured dialogue true to the late 19th Century.[5]

The script did establish the series format as seen on NBC that fall, introducing the character of George Taggart, the lawman played by Jack Elam, and the wary friendship between Taggart and Houston. There were structural problems with the script—it read more like a motion picture than it did a television story, for one thing—and the lead characters didn't have quite enough to do. But in speaking with reporters in August, Jack Webb gave Bellah credit for helping to develop the series.[6]

Webb also acknowledged the work cut out for his team as production got underway.

"This is a tough one," Jack Webb said. "But with the research we have we'll make it, and it will be good…Fortunately, Jeffrey Hunter had been wardrobed and costumed. Warner's been making westerns for years, and has six permanent western streets and a big back lot for location shots, plus tons of wardrobe. It was ideal for a quick turnaround."[7]

Speed was what was called for to make up for the late start. As Cecil Smith pointed out in *The Los Angeles Times* as the series went into production:

> It is imperative that production begins months before the air debut.
> It takes around six days to shoot an hour show and with the five-day
> work week, it is patently impossible to make such programs on the
> week-by-week basis they are shown.[8]

It was, perhaps, impossible. But Webb and Warner Brothers would come close to being the exception to the rule.

"We had done considerable research on the period in Texas," Webb said, "and the kind of cases a lawyer would be involved with."[9]

"Lawyering was considerably less disciplined in the early West than it is today," Hunter said. "It was a time when court judges and their entourages hopped from town to town to settle cases.

"Virtually every counselor had to be as colorful as the Jerry Giesler and Louis Nizers of this period."[10]

Webb and his producers went to work, giving Warner Bros. researchers the task of digging into legal cases of the early Southwest to provide the series with authenticity, with the idea of basing several episodes on actual cases.

All kinds of research was conducted, both before and after the signal from NBC to go into production; J. Marvin Hunter's 1951 book, *The Album of Gunfighters*, which featured historical photographs of well-known figures from western history, outlaws, and the like, was among the many books, magazines, and story collections scoured for story ideas. Other books consulted included *From Gun to Gavel: The Courtroom Recollections of James Mathers of Oklahoma* by Mathers and Marshall Houts, and *Murder and Mystery in New Mexico* by Erna Fegusson.

Some examples of these early story spring boards put forward included: basing an episode on a Texas Supreme Court ruling which required three Texas counties to conduct court proceedings in Spanish when jurors and other parties could not write or understand English; an episode in which Houston defends a member of a vigilante gang and loses the case; an episode about a Sister being asked to forgive the man who fatally wounded her brother; an episode utilizing Houston's famous 'fallen woman' speech; basing on episode on a real-life case in New Mexico in which a famous lawyer and his favorite child were murdered and the defendants acquitted; an episode based on the legalities involved in introducing liquor into the jury room during deliberations; and an episode about Houston using his wits to get a retrial for a client by firing shots into the ceiling of the court, scaring some jurors out of the courtroom, and then reminding the judge that jurors are not permitted to leave the court.[11]

Webb, Dackow and Meshekoff started hiring writers to compose the episodes they'd need in a hurry, including Anthony Ellis, Jack Usher, Shimon Wincelberg, E. M. Parsons, John Dunkel, Harry Kronman, John T. Dugan, Donald S. Sanford, Arthur Browne, Jr., and Jack Turley. The first scripts were needed in about a week's time.[12]

Jack Turley, specifically, was given the task of giving Bellah's script a rewrite. "'The Twisted Rope' had some problems attached to it. The original writer…turned in what proved to be an unacceptable script," Turley said.[13]

Jack Elam and guest star Victor Jory in "The Twisted Rope." *(Western TV Photos)*

Turley put more emphasis on the murder case and the legal entanglements and less focus on the recreation of a true-life old west atmosphere. Houston and Taggart were still wary of each other and, in fact, still engaged in a rousing fistfight, but on the whole the rewrite steered the series away from the dirty and dusty west of "Two Murders at Noon," while maintaining the action adventure style. *Variety* took note that "the interiors of the set in the first outing were much too spotless for the dusty western town portrayed."[14]

Turley punched the story up, making the murder victim a local sheriff rather than a local banker, and giving Houston a far more active role in the legal proceedings. Turley also built more television-style tension into the Acts, building to climaxes at the commercial breaks. Turley's rewrite was in these ways a big improvement.

Of course, not all scripts and story ideas would make it to the screen. John Dugan's "The County Seat Wars," for example, was never produced. His script centered on a strong-arm county sheriff in the newly formed Stark County, and the sheriff's plans to line his own pockets by charging outrageous taxes. The sheriff also schemes to establish the county seat in Kendall, where he has purchased a lot of property, as opposed to Woodward, in the script the "natural" spot for the seat. Involved in all of this is his lawyer, Temple Houston, who also falls in love with, and proposes to, the sheriff's daughter, before catching on to the sheriff's true intent.[15]

"It was done so fast the writers never had a chance to know what it was all about," Hunter said. "We all wanted to follow the line indicated by the pilot film, which we thought would make a charming series. NBC, however, favored making it serious."[16]

In developing scripts to shoot, Webb and Dackow were assisted by story consultant Thomas Thompson, who was supervising the preparation of scripts. Thompson had been associate producer on *Bonanza* the season before, and had written ten scripts for *Bonanza* and fourteen scripts for *Wagon Train*.

Webb, Dackow, Thompson, Hunter, and all the rest, were working morning, noon and night in those summer weeks to pull off this tremendous feat of television film production.

Associate producer Jimmy Lydon recalled the hectic start.

"Bill Conrad and I were the only contract producers on the lot," Lydon said. "When Webb called us into his office, he said, 'Fellas, I just sold *Temple Houston*. We gotta be on the air in four weeks...do it.'

"We were panicking because it was impossible to have scripts written and then shoot them, score them, dub them and deliver them to the network in four weeks!

"We called some very fast writers...they agreed and delivered us shootable scripts the following Friday. We put them into the mill right away and were shooting it Monday morning.

"We did all the preproduction work Saturday and Sunday. We shot two episodes together. We cut them, scored them, and I got a print of the first one out of the lab on a Friday night about 8:30 and in my car drove to L.A. airport and put it in the hands of a United Airlines captain who was taking the red-eye to New York.

"He carried it in the cockpit with him. At 6:30 in the morning when he arrived in New York, two (NBC) pages were waiting. He delivered the print to them and they ran it back to Manhattan and did what they had to do and we put it on the air that week. It was the wildest thing I've ever been involved in.

"We worked day and night...with preproduction, production, cutting, scoring, looping...the composer wrote a whole score for it in two days. We had the music orchestrated for a 50-piece orchestra in half a day. It was just incredible."[17]

The theme music for the series was done by Ned Washington and Frank Comstock, and was a variation of "The Yellow Rose of Texas." Frank Perkins also contributed to the music score for the series.

The fact that the series had an original theme was typical Warner Bros. practice in those years, but Warner Brothers for years had mostly relied upon the existing music in its library for use in the episodes of its television series, whether that series was a crime drama, western, or private eye show. The music came from outside sources or earlier Warner Bros productions.[18] In *Temple Houston* a viewer could occasionally hear variations of the series theme used in episodes; in "The Guardian," for example, the cue is played as Houston rides his horse.[19]

"The Twisted Rope," the first episode of *Temple Houston*, and for all intents and purposes the second pilot, went into production on August 7, 1963, and principal photography was completed on August 16. Studio veteran Abner Biberman directed Jack Turley's rewrite of Bellah's "Two Murders at Noon." Jack Webb and Mike Meshekoff were on set that first day to see how things went.

Somehow, through the high professionalism of all involved, the series premiere date of September 19th was met.

Incredible though it may seem, one episode, "The Third Bullet," began production on September 25th and finished on September 26th, the very next day.[20]

"Bill Conrad directed two scripts simultaneously at Warners," Jimmy Lydon said. "We bicycled Jeff and Elam between the two companies and Bill shot 'em both in four and a half days. Two complete one hour shows!"[21]

Columnist Terrence O'Flaherty visited the set in those first weeks, at a time when most series have several episodes in the can, but the newspaperman noted that *Temple Houston* was filming just its fourth episode. "Hunter is a genial sort of chap and seemed completely unruffled by the fact that the writers are handing out new pages of script. This has changed not only the lines but the condition of one of the principals, a character who supposed to be carrying a child being made unpregnant at the sudden change of a writer's pen."[22]

Producer Joe Dackow said Hunter and Elam were the saving graces of the show. "I've been in television since 1947," he said. "And I can't say enough about Jeff Hunter and Jack Elam…We've had to feed this pair two pages of script at a time because we've been working from the first draft.

"There's never been a complaint from either. Why, we've even had to make changes on a weekend, send new scripts to them on a Sunday night—and they've come in Monday morning with the changes memorized."[23]

Everyone put on a brave face, but there simply wasn't enough time. Scripts always need work, and often there's a better shot to get, but time was at a premium on the *Temple Houston* set. The need for wild scenes, additional scenes, to be shot, to help with story flow, was not uncommon.

The chaotic schedule did create problems beyond trying to simply find time to work out problems in the scripts. When still shots, to be used for publicity purposes, were taken on one of the western streets at Warner Brothers, for example, a car was clearly visible in the background in one of the shots.

The episodes being produced also reflected the network's preference for a serious tone. In "The Twisted Rope," Houston has to clear two brothers of a murder charge by exposing their own sister as the killer, even though she has cared for them their entire lives, to the sacrifice of her own emotional well-being; in "Gallows in Galilee" he must deal with a 'hanging judge,' and in "Find Angel Chavez" he must clear Taggart of a murder charge.

For all of the running around, late script changes, long hours, and production challenges, the set of *Temple Houston* was mostly a happy one.

"From the day we started, through the whole 26 episodes, we never had a harsh word," Jack Elam said of his work on the series with Jeff Hunter. "Sometimes, I know I can get to be a pain in the neck, but Hunter was a great guy and he had a lot of clout with NBC. He ran the show, but he never played the role about it at all."[24]

Old West law, Warner Bros. style.
(Western TV Photos)

Director Alvin Ganzer, who directed the two-day episode "The Third Bullet," said Hunter was a joy to work with on the show. "He was a pleasant guy, easy to work with, and a good, solid actor who never gave you any trouble."[25]

"He was the nicest guy on the set," Van Williams said. "He never argued about anything, took all the direction."[26]

Not that everything was peace and harmony. Jack Turley remembered the chaos surrounding his script for the first episode.

"After I rewrote Bellah's script," Turley said, "the changes began to cascade onto me like an avalanche out of control. The series was new at that time and everybody on the production team saw an opportunity to add their own imprint by trying to grab a piece of the writing credit.

"Fortunately, The Writer's Guild solved the problem through arbitration and only the original writer (Bellah) ended up with a shared credit—even though I had totally rewritten his script in what is called a 'Page one rewrite.' It's the nature of the business. The original writer is usually protected, even if his writing bombs."[27]

As the series episodes started to air, reaction started to come in. "The Twisted Rope" received mixed reviews.

Variety noted that the "Preem episode of NBC-TV's *Temple Houston* tried to mix many elements in the old oater form, but came out with neither a fast paced actioner, nor an absorbing, if slowly developed character study.

"It was more of a mish-mash of derivative things, borrowed from Zane Grey, *Perry Mason*, and Freud...it was a ho-hum outing, hardly the series which might spell the turns of WB's fortunes on network TV, which is low at this point." [28]

Cynthia Lowry of *The Associated Press* agreed, writing, "It was neither a good western nor a suspenseful courtroom drama."[29]

The Los Angeles Times at least acknowledged the time crunch the series was under. "*Temple Houston* really isn't bad," Walt Dutton wrote, "considering the producers did not expect to have the show on the air this season and had to throw the first episodes together in a hurry. Were it not for overstatement it might have been an hour of passable entertainment."

Dutton described the series as "sagebrush *Perry Mason*" and said "Hunter and Elam were adequate in their roles."[30]

On the plus side, *The Hollywood Reporter* was more favorable, saying, "Of the new season's shows to date, *Temple Houston* looks like the one to beat. A big, slick frontier action drama, this has quality in every frame of film in the best Warners tradition… If "The Twisted Rope" sets a pattern, viewers will stay glued to the sets as bloodthirsty action opens the segment, gives way to tense realism, and ends on a piece of gripping logic.

"The good looks and talent of Jeffrey Hunter…will make his 'Houston' an odds-on favorite…Jack Elam's unique ability gives just the needed complement."[31]

The Chicago Tribune said the series had a chance to be one of the hits of the season. "It has got everything that an epic of the southwest seems to need—murder and mayhem, frontier fights, hair pulling, slugging, heavy breathing, bad grammar, dogs barking at sundown, and roosters crowing at dawn…this hour long newcomer will go over big with all those who demand action, adventure, violence, and suspense in their television fare."[32]

But then and now, the networks lived and died on ratings. In 1963, the first important look at the ratings for network programs came in October, when the first national Nielsen ratings of the season were released. The ratings were compiled from tape-recording machines attached to televisions in about 900 homes.

The series never found its audience. The ratings were made public during the last week of October, and there was no good news for *Temple Houston*. Of the season's 32 new programs, *Temple Houston* ranked 31st, and it barely registered in the ratings of all the shows on the air.[33]

The shows up against the Hunter program were some of the most popular on television, like *The Donna Reed Show*, which was the tenth most popular program in the country. *Temple Houston* was being regularly bested by all of the shows it was competing against, like *Rawhide*, *The Flintstones* and *Password*.

Preemptions didn't help. In several markets the program was shifted away from Thursday night at 7:30 to other time slots (in the Spokane, WA market, for example, the show was played at 6:30 pm on Saturdays). In some of the country's biggest media markets, including Boston, the show was often pre-empted or simply didn't air at all.

Another factor might have been that it was a difficult time in network television history to launch a western. The western genre had lost its top ranking in the primetime ratings. In 1959, Westerns provided almost eighteen hours of programming a week; in 1963, that number was down to about seven. As the 1960s progressed, the only new western on network television to last longer than a year or two was *The Big Valley*, which aired on ABC from 1965- 69.

Perhaps it would have helped to shoot in color instead of black and white (although that would have rendered much of Warner Brothers' stock footage of cattle drives, wagon trains, etc., useless to the series).

Hunter tried to be philosophical about the ratings. He noted that they were based on a 30-city basis and that the show was seen in only 22 of those markets. The series, he knew, was airing in 136 markets around the country; 40 of those were Nielsen rated cities.

But, generally speaking, there was no disguising the fact that the show, in ratings terms, was a bomb. Even less scientific polling methods didn't bode well for the series. In Houston, a television writer for *The Houston Chronicle* polled about 400 readers on the season's new television shows, and *Temple Houston* was one of the five most disliked new shows. There were rumors that the show would be pulled off the air.[34]

The ratings generated an immediate meeting at NBC to talk about what might be done to give the series a boost. Advertising, publicity, and promotions personnel from the network and Warner brothers met on October 31st. They discussed a heavy promotional campaign, which, schedules permitting, could include:

1. Hunter being flown to New York on November 23rd for a week of "concentrated promotional activities" such as appearing on various network shows, including *The Tonight Show*, the *Today Show*, and the Thanksgiving Day parade. Newspaper, magazine, and television interviews would be arranged;

2. On Friday, November 15th, Hunter being flown to the Broadcasters Promotion Association's convention in San Francisco. Interviews in the local press would be arranged;

3. Jack Elam appearing on NBC's *Your First Impression* and *You Don't Say*, both taped in Burbank;

4. On New Year's Day, Hunter appearing in the NBC broadcast box during the airing of the Pasadena Rose Parade.[35]

Some of these ideas panned out, other did not. Jack Webb was the one who went to San Francisco, for example, where he told the convention that, "The first obligation of the television producer should be to make his show taut with believability."[36]

In the meantime, NBC had decided to stay with the series. For one thing, the fan mail poured in for Jeff Hunter, despite the ratings, and that provided a little hope the ratings might turn around; for another, the network didn't have another show ready, anyway.[37]

Behind the scenes, Hunter campaigned for a return to the humor found in the show's original format. Jack Webb, it should be said, objected to the change—he had decided that he preferred the serious approach. Finally, about dozen episodes into the season, NBC agreed to the change.

"NBC picked up the option for us to do 22 shows," Hunter said. "So there's hope we will go the full season, maybe longer. The network has been very good about refusing to panic.

"I believe things will be getting better, especially with the new approach to the show."[38]

Oddly enough, the show's late start in August actually helped the producers change course when it was decided to do so. Cecil Smith of *The Los Angeles Times* described the usual course of events in 1963 network television as a game of roulette:

> It's in the nature of modern television that by the time a new series reaches the air and is exposed to any sort of public or critical reaction, it will have been committed to the extent of 10 or 12 or more episodes already filmed…furthermore, once a show hits the air with the product it has, there is almost nothing that can be done to change it if the first reaction is bad...
>
> Whatever you show in January, you live or die by what you had on the air in October, and what you had in October was probably shot in May.[39]

In the case of *Temple Houston*, of course, there was no such problem because there was no backlog of episodes. The low-rated series did not have to live with episodes already produced and ready for air. In that limited sense, the switch was simpler for *Temple Houston* to make than it would have been for another series, although there was the usual scrambling on scripts.

"I think it's a much better show this way," Hunter said, "And certainly it's easier for me to do. Doing an hour-long show with a lot of courtroom dialogue is tough enough. It's worse if you have to do heavy dramatics.

"About the ninth show I began to drag and I didn't see how I could get my energy up again. But now that I can play it lighter I'm getting my stride."[40]

On the air, the change officially arrived with the "Fracas at Kiowa Flats" episode broadcast on December 12th, although "Dark Madonna," filmed earlier, was still to air that month. *TV Guide*'s episode description for "Fracas" said the episode "marks a change of format for the series, which now assumes a tongue-in-cheek approach." Another television writer noted that the series was "trying to be another *Maverick*."[41]

The return of the lighter touch wasn't the only change in the format. Eventually, a set of recurring characters was added to the cast, including James Best as Gotch, Mary Wickes as Ida Goff, and Frank Ferguson as Judge Gurney, as Houston and Taggart called one town, Lindley, home.

Television writers did not greet the format change necessarily enthusiastically. UPI's Rick DuBrow, for one, wrote that, "Not long ago, *Temple Houston* decided to stop playing its stories straight, which, considering its leading man, was an act of courage unmatched since NBC put the series on in the first place."[42]

Van Williams said that critics of the time often missed an important point when writing about series leads. "The problem with being a leading man in those days," he said, "was that the acting was going on all around you and you were reacting. They didn't get you all that involved."[43]

"The Fracas at Kiowa Flats,"
with guest star Kathie Browne.
(Western TV Photos)

The format change didn't mean that the production challenges would improve for the actors and crew. "Ten Rounds for Baby" was shot in just three days in January. Van Williams was a guest star in that episode. "Oh my God," he recalled. "I don't know how they got it ready that fast."[44]

With pick-up shots and post-recording, Hunter at times was working on three episodes at once.

Behind the scenes, there had been changes in the ranks, as Richard Bluel came over from similar duties on *Bonanza* to replace Joseph Dackow as supervising producer, and the Jack Webb saga was coming to its conclusion; he was fired in December from his post as head of television at Warner Brothers, just about the time the series format was changing. His objections to the format reversal didn't help his cause.

In November, Warner Brothers also announced its intention to release the first pilot to theaters in an attempt to recoup at least some of its investment, and perhaps giving the show a boost in the process. Now retitled *The Man from Galveston*, and featuring dialogue editing that changed Temple Houston's name to Timothy Higgins, the 57-minute film was released to theaters in December and January as part of double bills. *Variety* said that while the pilot was successful at selling the series, "as a theatrical feature…(the film) is mighty skimpy fare—barely acceptable as a running mate."[45]

The New York Times was no kinder: "It's pretty much the same cliché-ridden show, with Jeff (formerly Jeffrey) Hunter broadly depicting the rambunctious legal trickster and solving a murder in court to bring to a climax a not very mystifying melodramatic plot.

"The acting is routine, the sets are reminiscent of *Cheyenne*, the technique is in the clumsiest television style, and the audience mentality aimed at is obviously 12."[46]

The reviews demonstrated the problem in releasing television fare to the big screen domestically, where the expectations were higher. The original plan had been better; if the pilot was not to be used as an individual episode, then release it overseas, with added footage.

The release certainly didn't do Hunter's big screen career any favors; the film had a cheap feel to it, playing as the second half of a double bill. It was nothing that was going to build big picture momentum, extra pay day or not.

Besides, viewers were staying away from the series in droves on NBC; it's hard to understand what would have possessed anyone to think patrons would pay to see it in the movie theater. It was merely an attempt—an understandable one—to at least recoup some of the costs.

But no matter what was tried, viewers just didn't seem interested. Of the format switch, Hunter said simply, "It was too late."[47]

The negative reviews remained highly so. Hal Humphrey, writing in *The Los Angeles Times* in late December, gave the series one of his annual "Ten Worst TV Awards" in the category of 'Worst Adventure Series.' Humphrey wrote, "*Redigo* (NBC), *Temple Houston* (NBC), and *Greatest Show on Earth* (ABC) share a three-way tie for ridiculous stories and the most over-acting since *East Lynne*."[48]

At the network program meetings in January 1964, NBC officially cancelled the show, although the network did decide to allow a full slate of new episodes, twenty-six, to be produced. New episodes aired through April 2nd, and repeats through September.

One production member told *The New York Times*, "I don't think viewers want their myths mixed. The West must remain the West—for Indians, pioneers, and cowboys."[49] Not for lawyers, presumably.

Asked about the series in months to come, Jeffrey Hunter could at times only shake his head, thinking about the rushed production schedule, the format changes, the pressures on all involved, the lack of time to work on scripts, the production issues, and what might have been.

"The big joke around town was that it was about a synagogue in Texas," he said. "It must have really confused the viewers."[50]

§

ENDNOTES

1. Letter agreements between Jeffrey Hunter and Warner Bros. Pictures, June 20, 1963, August 1, 1963; Boverman memo to Moore, June 27, 1963, Warner Bros. Archives, University of Southern California, Los Angeles.
2. Terry, page F 13
3. Pruess, page 29
4. "Two Murders at Noon," written by James Warner Bellah, James Warner Bellah Collection, Howard Gotlieb Archival Research Center, Boston University, Boston, MA.
5. Ibid
6. Smith, "Better Late than never for Webb," sec 4, page 12.
7. Ibid, and Lowry, "Jack Webb Finds Spot in Fall TV for Lawyer Show," page 12 A.
8. Smith, "New Shows Play Russian Roulette," page D 12.
9. Lowry, "Jack Webb Finds Spot in Fall TV for Lawyer Show," page 12 A.
10. "Frontier Lawyer Had to be Colorful," page 6 B
11. Temple Houston Research file, various memos, Warner Bros. Archives, University of Southern California, Los Angeles.
12. "Ten Writers Plotting NBC Legal Series," V, page 11.
13. Turley, letter, April 1, 1994.
14. *Variety,* September 25, 1963.
15. "The County Seat Wars," written by John T. Dugan, Warner Bros. Archive, University of Southern California, Los Angeles.
16. Spiro, "Happy in Hollywood," page 4
17. *Western Clippings,* page 8
18. Burlingame, page 41.
19. The second half of this episode was acquired on video, collector to collector, for home viewing.
20. *Temple Houston* production files, Warner Bros. Archives, University of Southern California, Los Angeles.
21. *Western Clippings,* page 8.

22. O' Flaherty, "How Green Was My Money," page 41.

23. "TV Scout Reports," page 3 B

24. *Western Clippings,* page 8.

25. Ganzer, interview.

26. Williams, interview.

27. Turley, letter, April 1, 1994.

28. *Variety,* September 25, 1963.

29. Lowry, "Temple Houston Could Be Guilty," page 7.

30. Dutton, page B 3

31. Porter, *The Hollywood Reporter,* September 23, 1963.

32. Wolters, page C 10.

33. Gould, various articles, *The New York Times,* October 28- 31, 1963.

34. Smith, "After Rites, Tonight's Bright," sec. V, page 14.

35. Meeting notes, Warner Bros. Archives, The University of Southern California, Los Angeles.

36. O'Flaherty, "Return of Dum-De-Dum-Dum," page 45.

37. Grant, "Robert Vaughn Wants to Quit 'Lieutenant,'" page 7 B.

38. Thomas, "Shift to Comedy May Save Show," page 7

39. Smith, "New Shows Play Russian Roulette," page D 12.

40. Thomas, "Shift to Comedy May Save Show," page 7.

41. *TV Guide,* December 12, 1963; *The Los Angeles Times,* IV, page 10.

42. DuBrow, page 5.

43. Williams, interview.

44. Ibid.

45. *Variety,* January 15, 1964.

46. *The New York Times,* January 23, 1964, 26:3.

47. Terry, page F 13.

48. Humphrey, page B 23

49. Gardner, X: 17.

50. Terry, page F 13

Chapter Four
Jeffrey Hunter as Temple Houston

The Warner Brothers series prospectus for *Temple Houston* described the lead character as a traditional Western hero. Temple Houston was courageous, tenacious, and smart. But the series developers also wanted Houston to be compassionate, and passionate about the events transpiring around him. Houston was to have a strong ethical sense of right and wrong, and the courage of his convictions.

Temple Houston was described as someone who could ride, shoot, fight, drink, and love with the best of them, and maybe better than most. The modesty that he displays in day-to-day life would disappear as soon as he enters a courtroom, becoming the flamboyant attorney famous throughout the American Southwest.[1]

Houston was, to turn an oft-used phrase in the Western, a larger than life character. In Warner Bros. terms, the character was as tough as Cheyenne and as glib as Maverick—a new kind of western hero, the studio hoped.

"There are many sides to his character," Hunter said. "He was a flamboyant orator, he was a bit of a dandy, he was tough, he was gentle, he was an excellent marksman…which gives us considerable latitude within a western format."[2]

Potentially, the character would be an interesting and complex one to play. To carry the show, and to appear in as many scenes as he was scheduled to, Hunter would need to call upon his many years of experience as an actor, in and out of Westerns, to make the part, and the series, a success.

Henry Herman McKinnies, Jr. was born in New Orleans, La., on November 25, 1926. He grew up in the Milwaukee, Wisconsin area, taking part in local theatre, radio, and television productions, and playing a lot of sports at Whitefish Bay High School. He had an interest in acting in college at Northwestern University, after finishing a hitch in the Navy, but he majored in speech and radio. Upon graduation in 1949, he enrolled in graduate school at UCLA.

"Hank" was planning on a career in radio and perhaps teaching when a talent scout spotted him at UCLA in a production of *All My Sons*. He signed with Twentieth Century Fox in 1950, eventually taking the Hollywood name of Jeffrey Hunter. That initial contract would lead to parts in nearly forty motion pictures during the 1950s and early 1960s, everything from *Fourteen Hours* to *A Kiss Before Dying* and *No Down Payment*, leading up to *Temple Houston*. In those years Hunter became well known in Hollywood and well-liked by movie fans.

"He was a very warm, decent, down to earth human being," actor and co-star George Takei said.[1]

"Jeffrey Hunter was always down to earth," Van Williams said. "I had a lot of respect for him. He was one of the few friends I had in the acting business."[2]

Hunter's personal life included three marriages. His first wife was actress Barbara Rush (1950–55); his second was the former model Joan Bartlett (1957–1967); his third wife was actress Emily McLaughlin (1969), famous as Nurse Jessie Brewer on daytime television's *General Hospital*.

Jeffrey Hunter was not a man who relished inactivity. He had ambitions beyond the world of acting. At various times, his outside business interests included a ski lodge, a documentary film company,[3] fiber-glass bottom boats, and a business management firm.

He was hard on himself. "Never mind this baby face of mine," Hunter told *TV Guide*. "I've got a healthy actor's ego, even though I don't go around putting it on display. I don't throw things. I don't yell at people...

"...And then when I get off alone I'll work off the rage that's boiling inside—I'll do push-ups or chin-ups on a door. Ten push-ups, 20 pull-ups and I simmer down."[4]

Jeffrey Hunter was certainly no stranger to westerns when he agreed to play the role of Temple Houston on television. In fact, he was quite familiar with the genre, and some of his best roles had come in Westerns. Tall, handsome, and blue-eyed, Hunter looked every inch the Western hero, and over the years leading up to the *Temple Houston* series he had played a wide variety of western roles.

"He did a lot of stuff at 20th Century Fox that I thought was very good," actor and friend Van Williams said. "He did all those westerns, a lot of work over there."[5]

The Westerns in the first decade of Hunter's career included *Three Young Texans* (1953); *White Feather, Seven Angry Men* (1955); *The Proud Ones, The Searchers*,

The Great Locomotive Chase, Gun for a Coward (1956); *The True Story of Jesse James* (1957), as Frank James; and *Sergeant Rutledge* (1960), in which Hunter played a Western lawyer for the first time.

Director John Ford was in many ways the actor's mentor; Ford cast Hunter in three of his films, including the pivotal role of Martin Pawley in *The Searchers*, the young man who travels with Ethan Edwards (John Wayne) for seven years in search of a young girl kidnapped by Indians.

During one of the first few days of filming, Ford pulled the young actor aside and told him to stop acting, and to start feeling the part. Hunter would tell the story to friends and reporters for years.

Temple Houston was one of Hunter's many Western roles.
(Milton T. Moore Photos)

While Hunter would perhaps receive more attention for, and is perhaps best remembered for, his role as Jesus in *King of Kings*, a role Ford recommended him for, Hunter's most important film performance is in *The Searchers*. Take this film away from his career, and you take away momentum that propelled Hunter to years as a popular and dedicated leading man. Hunter called the film his "personal favorite."[6]

For Ford's *Sergeant Rutledge* (1960), scriptwriters James Warder Bellah and Willis Goldbeck had written a cavalry story they first called "Captain Buffalo." The script focused on a liberated slave and cavalry officer, Braxton Rutledge, who is put on trial for the rape and murder of a white girl.

Ford chose Hunter to play the officer and lawyer-advocate who defended Rutledge, Lt. Thomas Cantrell, while Constance Towers was selected to play Mary Beecher, Cantrell's love interest. Woody Strode was cast as Rutledge. The race issue was provocative for its time, but in many other ways the picture was a typically rousing John Ford cavalry picture. "One of the best pictures I ever made," Hunter said.[7]

The actor felt that Ford understood him, and knew how to prod him into his best work. The memories of *The Searchers*, *The Last Hurrah*, and *Sergeant Rutledge* were strong and overwhelmingly positive.

From the set of *King of Kings* in August, 1960, Hunter wrote to Ford, "Should every thought of you these past months have been set on paper I'm sure you would have several volumes by now...

As Martin Pawley in John Ford's *The Searchers*, 1956.

"First, I want you to know that I know you are responsible for my role in *King of Kings*. And what an awkward moment for me, trying once again to express in some fashion my gratitude for all of the many wonderful things you have done for me since the beginning; your belief, your patient understanding, your inspiration and your love.

"What can I say except that I love you deeply and hope that I can and will measure up to your expectations. I realize I have much to learn and I promise you that I'll continue to improve my craftsmanship in every way I know how."[8]

Ford and the young actor had developed a very close personal relationship during the filming of *The Searchers*. Hunter would always remember what Ford had done for him, and taught him. From *The Searchers* sprang his friendship with Ford and subsequently the opportunity to do his best work in films.

"The greatest acting compliment I ever had was when director John Ford borrowed me three times," Hunter said.[9]

The years from 1956–1962 comprise the period representing Hunter's highest visibility and his best work in film. His films included Ford's *The Last Hurrah*, with Hunter as a young reporter whose uncle is a wily old politician; *The True Story of Jesse James*, directed by Nicholas Ray; *Sergeant Rutledge*; *Key Witness*, about a family terrorized by a gang; *The Longest Day*, with Hunter as an heroic soldier at Normandy; and *Man-Trap*, a crime film based on a John D. MacDonald novel. He was receiving thousands of fan letters a month.

Also in this group is a film that deserves special attention, *Hell to Eternity*.

The film was based on the true story of Guy Gabaldon, a Marine who became a hero during the World War II battle to capture Saipan. Helped by his ability to speak Japanese fluently (he had been raised by Japanese foster parents in the United States), Gabaldon brought in hundreds of prisoners on his own.

"I very much admired him for taking on the lead role in *Hell to Eternity*," George Takei, who co-starred in the film, said. "Many people in Hollywood were skittish about the role—the film was one of the first, I believe, to deal with the internment of Japanese-Americans in World War II. Having Jeffrey Hunter in the lead helped a great deal to promote the film."[10]

On television, Hunter had appeared in network anthology shows before playing two biographical roles in Westerns. The first was as the explorer John Charles Fremont in a live NBC broadcast in January 1960 of the series *Our American Heritage* called "Destiny, West!" and the second was as the humanitarian Dr. Walter Reed in a 1962 episode of *Death Valley Days* called "Suzie." Each of these television appearances used the Hunter image as "the good guy" to help tell its story; for example, as Reed, Hunter helps to rescue a young girl whose parents—one white, the other Indian— have been killed in an Indian raid. In doing so he resists a suggestion that the girl be abandoned because she's "a half-breed."[11]

And then there was *King of Kings*.

Westerns and other work notwithstanding, the place to start in understanding Jeffrey Hunter's Hollywood career, and what led him to *Temple Houston*, is in Spain, in 1960, during the several months the actor was part of the crew making MGM's 1961 blockbuster, *King of Kings*. Front and center in the film, and its subsequent controversy, was Jeffrey Hunter.

Hunter didn't speak very much while making the picture, though he'd never been known in Hollywood as a snob. Rather, he had so devoted himself to the role and the film that he felt better prepared if he stayed in the part. He would stand quietly off to one side, or studying his lines in his dressing room, waiting for the film to roll.

"I really chose him for his eyes," producer Sam Bronston said of Hunter at the time. "It was important that the man playing Christ should have memorable eyes.

"This film was a great responsibility…Jeff took the part very seriously. He had great presence."[12]

Hunter trained and studied diligently for it; and he went out of his way to ensure that neither publicists nor the press would exploit his part in the film.

Hunter took steps to ensure that dignity would surround his participation in *King of Kings*. "I made a point not to smoke, or appear in any way undignified. This wasn't really an effort on my part. It just seemed right."[13]

The Sermon on the Mount scene in *King of Kings* is a memorable moment in film history. Director Nicholas Ray shot the sequence in the hillside outside the village of Venta de Frascuela, Spain, utilizing the services of thousands of extras along with the main characters performing the scene. The scene took five days to shoot, and lasts fifteen minutes in the film.

The scene required Hunter to move among thousands of extras, who had been recruited from nearby villages, fielding questions and giving answers. The camera crew laid more than 300 feet of camera tracks down the side of the mountain, in places at a 58-degree angle. The scene required 81 different camera set-ups to complete.[14]

In some motion pictures of the period, such as *Ben Hur,* Christ's face wasn't even shown. Christ in *King of Kings,* however, was anything but an off-screen character.

"We had hundreds of extras when we went to Pino Sierra, a little town a half hour from Madrid to film the Sermon on the Mount," Hunter told columnist Louella Parsons. "The natives were all assembled before I appeared saying the Beatitudes, and people fell on their knees, crossed themselves, and some of them were hysterical in their emotions.

"We had to explain it was just a motion picture, and Christ's appearance was made before He was crucified, and actually before Christianity was born."[15]

"The Spanish extras were impossible to handle with him around," Sam Bronston said in 1973. "We'd spend a day trying to get a simple shot and then Jeffrey would walk out and all the extras would fall to their knees. They actually believed he was Christ. A difficult load for a man to bear."[16]

Friends and fellow actors warned Jeffrey Hunter to stay away from the role as Jesus in *King of Kings.* They feared it would have a disastrous impact on his career, derailing all of the effort he'd made to be seen as more than just a handsome star; they told him the tale of actor H.B. Warner, who had played the part in a 1927 silent picture for Cecil B. DeMille, and supposedly complained for years afterward that his career was never the same again.

Undeterred, Hunter accepted the role with enthusiasm and excitement. He was truly honored by the opportunity. "These three months in Spain seem more like three weeks," Hunter said when he wrote a letter to Ford in August, 1960. "…The experience of playing this part has some incredible moments."[17]

"In Jeffrey was an honest warmth which came across on the screen," director Nicholas Ray said. "I think he was superb as Christ."[18]

Van Williams attended the premiere of the film. "I saw him in it, and I thought he was great," the actor said. "I went up to him at the end of the movie and gave him a big hug, and we're both sitting there crying, and he's saying, 'I can't cry, I can't cry.'"[19]

Not all critics were kind to the actor following the release of *King of Kings*; the unkindest cut was certainly found in *Time* magazine, which said in an unsigned review, "…incontestably the corniest, phoniest, ickiest, and most monstrously vulgar of all the big Bible stories Hollywood has told in the last decade…

"Whatever possessed producer Bronston and director Ray to offer the part to Jeffrey Hunter, 35, a fan-mag cover boy with a flabby face, a cute little lopsided smile, baby blue eyes and barely enough historic ability to play a Hollywood marine?...

"The definitive criticism of Bronston's Christ, and indeed of his entire film, is expressed in the snide subtitle by which it is widely known in the trade: 'I Was a Teenage Jesus.'"[20]

Moira Walsh, writing in the Jesuit weekly *America* said, "...the culmination of a gigantic fraud perpetuated by the film industry on the movie going public...Christ is there as a physical presence, but his spirit is absent..."[21]

It's not that this sort of review was the norm upon the release of the film; generally speaking, many of its reviews were pretty good. As is often the case, the film received its share of both good and bad reviews.

Bosley Crowther, in *The New York Times*, wrote that, "Mr. Hunter wears his make-up nobly and performs with simplicity and taste."[22]

Robert Landry, reviewing the film for *Variety*, lauded the production, and liked Hunter's performance. "Carefully, reverently and beautifully made," he wrote, and called it "a major motion picture by any standard." On Hunter's performance as Jesus, Landry said, "Did he not carry conviction one may only imagine the embarrassment. But he does come remarkably close to being ideal."[23]

Philip Hartung, writing in *Commonweal*, was an example of a reviewer who thought Hunter worked in the part. "On the whole, Jeffrey Hunter looks convincing in the title role and plays it with a reverence and stern simplicity that are quite effective...it is unfortunate that his voice...doesn't have a more inspired quality."[24]

Hartung's critique of the film itself was consistent with what many critics said. "Jesus emerges not as the Living Christ, the Son of God, but as an inspired leader," he wrote.[25] Some reviewers felt too many liberties had been taken with biblical stories, that the producers should not have cast a divorced man as Jesus, and so on.

The trade paper *Variety* tried to make some sense out of the criticism being fired on the film. The paper noted that the picture was being burned by "unexplained resentment and attack.

"...there may be a tendency to unload on *King of Kings* a backlogged resentment against earlier and perhaps too many biblical releases.

"...many who have never attended church are among the most opinionated...it's a literal, not a facetious, point that the New Testament has suddenly become New York cocktail party conversation...some of the cocktail party critics may be forced to the extreme of reading the Bible again to gain weight for their arguments."[26]

The film may not as been as striking as other epic films of the time such as *Ben Hur* or *Spartacus*, but it clearly entertained and fascinated audiences around the world. Its box office upon its first release was $6.5 million—less than what MGM was hoping for, but potent nonetheless.[27]

The film enjoyed a better reputation in subsequent years, in some respects, than when it was released.

Still, Sam Bronston would wonder, years later, about the impact the film had on Hunter's life. "That poor man," he said. "Drunks would come up to him in nightclubs and tell him to perform miracles. He was hounded and never let alone. He couldn't go anywhere."[28]

Bronston said he thought the film "disintegrated" Hunter's career.[29]

That may be overstating the problem to some extent, but a story from the set of a television production in which Hunter starred is illuminating.

In 1961, Hunter starred in "The Trial," the pilot for what was described as a "forthcoming" television anthology series from Four Star Television about the history of the nation's universities. The series was to be called *The Equitable Life Theatre*, after its sponsor, and Walter Pidgeon would serve as host. In the pilot, directed by Joe Pevney, Hunter played Father Edward Sorin, the founder of the University of Notre Dame in 1842.

But on the set, someone trying to be funny yelled to the actor, "Kind of a comedown, huh, Jeff?"[30]

The 'comedown,' if that's what it was, wasn't in Hunter's performance in the show—in fact, he was quite good as Father Sorin, and the story, about the struggles that faced the group of Catholic priests who built Notre Dame from scratch, was compelling. The story was one of courage, and tolerance, and was a worthy one to tell, be it on the big or small screen.

Hunter's work in 1961 consisted of television appearances in the Four Star pilot (which unfortunately never aired), an appearance on the television series *Checkmate*, the lead role in the film *Man-Trap*, and one of the many supporting roles in *The Longest Day*, Darryl F. Zanuck's film on D-Day in World War II.

The point wasn't, and isn't, to denigrate any of these projects. Hunter was very good in all of them, and he was working. What was missing was another big part in a major motion picture follow-up to *King of Kings*.

On into 1962, Hunter kept busy, and was cast as the lead (and again was very good) in the 1962 World War II drama *No Man is an Island*, a favorite of Hunter's among his film performances, but here again—while the film was very entertaining, and included Hunter's name above the title, old-fashioned Hollywood style, it wasn't a film that could be classified as a big budget, big cast follow-up to a major film like *King of Kings*. *Gold for the Caesars*, subsequently released by MGM, was filmed in Italy in the fall of 1962. Hunter called it his "first toga role," and it was an early preview of the European film phase of Hunter's career that, unknown to him, was on the horizon.[31]

"I'll guarantee you," Van Williams said, "after that movie, I'm sure he lost a lot of roles that people were thinking about him for, and they said, 'We can't use him, he was Jesus Christ. Everybody's going to think, hey, that's Jesus Christ, we can't believe him in that role.' I saw it happen to many, many people in that business."[32]

Hunter remained an absolutely popular actor, and his popularity with audiences led to steady employment in a variety of interesting roles, especially on television, in the months before *Temple Houston* premiered in 1963, but a major film star, like some of the people who came into Hollywood at about the same time as he did—a Charlton Heston, or a Rock Hudson—he was not.

"There is a certain amount of luck involved," director Alvin Ganzer said.[33]

Part of the reason Hunter took on the lead role in a weekly television series is because the lead roles in A-list films didn't materialize after *King of Kings*.

Hunter insisted over the years, at least publicly, that he was not typecast by the part. He was asked about the film repeatedly; it is the rare published Jeffrey Hunter interview that does not make mention of *King of Kings*. As *Temple Houston* premiered, many of the newspaper profiles of Hunter carried the theme that had had "defied 'jinx' in film role."[34]

Even later, with the release of George Stevens' *The Greatest Story Ever Told* in 1965, Hunter found himself being asked about *King of Kings* all over again.

"Actors insisted I would be typed," he said. "On the contrary, I believe the part gave impetus to my acting career."[35]

Hunter pointed to roles past and present for proof of this. In 1964, he played a parolee testing the faith of a nun as he considers committing a crime in an episode of *Bob Hope Presents the Chrysler Theatre*, and in 1965, he would appear in *Brainstorm* as an unbalanced scientist; as a Mexican bandit in the filmed-in-Spain *Murieta*; as a criminal hunted by *The FBI* in the premiere of that long-running television series; and as a friend in need of a favor from an old college chum in the "The Trains of Silence" episode of *Kraft Suspense Theater*.

The actor's performance in *King of Kings*, while not Oscar worthy, certainly didn't merit the personal attacks, whatever one may have thought about the picture. Audiences around the world reacted positively to him in the film, and he had the letters to prove it. "It was a satisfying and wonderful experience," he said in 1964. "I still get 1,500 letters a month from all over the world. Beautiful, beautiful letters.

"People write telling me what the picture meant to them, how it gave them a visual picture of Christ, how moved they were."[36]

"There are some things," Hunter said, "That can't be measured in dollars and cents."[37]

Hunter tried to manage the experience as best he could, both the critics and the fans. Of the critics, he once said, "I don't mind criticism, if it's well founded. But criticism should be directed at the role, not the person."[38]

A gallery of television roles—as Dr. Walter Reed in *Death Valley Days* and Captain Christopher Pike (with Susan Oliver as Vina) in *Star Trek: The Cage* (Star Trek *photo courtesy of Paramount Pictures)* ...

... and as criminals in *The FBI* (1965) and *Bob Hope Presents the Chrysler Theatre* (1964). *(Milton T. Moore photos)*

The career bumps were part of the reason Jeff Hunter took the lead role of *Temple Houston.* He was doing the best he could with the parts he was offered, and he genuinely enjoyed working in television. He had high hopes for the series when he signed with Warner Bros.

There were those around him who told him to avoid television, that he was a movie star, not a weekly television leading man or "special guest star." But Hunter knew better. "I've gotten some of my best chances in television," he said in 1963. "The parts have been unique and varied."[39]

Hunter had strong connections to three other television series projects. His experiences in them help to demonstrate the ups and downs of network television.

Several months after *Temple Houston* ended in 1964, Hunter starred in what is now a famous television pilot, the very first *Star Trek* ever made.

Star Trek at this time was not the multi-million dollar phenomenon it was to become in later decades. In 1964, the entirety of *Star Trek* consisted of a series format and a pilot script written by creator Gene Roddenberry, who had been writing for television for years, most prominently for the western *Have Gun, Will Travel.*

As Desilu Studios made preparations for its *Star Trek* pilot, the names of more than forty actors were on the list of possibilities for the lead role, the captain of a futuristic spaceship exploring outer space, including Jeffrey Hunter.

Like any other film or television project, the casting of the role was a combination of actor availability, interest on the part of the performer, network approval, and bottom line business.

In the end, the role of Captain Christopher Pike went to Jeffrey Hunter.

Desilu's Herbert F. Solow said the network, the studio, and the producers were thrilled to get the actor. While *Temple Houston* had failed, they knew that Hunter was aware of the daily grind of putting out a series. *Star Trek* was going to be an extremely complex series to produce, in many ways the first of its kind, and experience on the set of a network series was going to be crucial.[40]

Desilu filmed this first *Star Trek* adventure over sixteen days in late 1964. By all accounts, Hunter very much enjoyed his time in the *Star Trek* universe; his enthusiasm for the project was clear in comments he made about *Star Trek* to a writer in January 1965.

"We run into pre-historic worlds, contemporary societies, and civilizations far more developed than our own," he said. "It's a great format because writers have a free hand—they can have us land on a monster-infested planet, or deal in human relations involving the large number of people who live together on this gigantic ship.

"...It will be an hour long, in color with a regular cast of a half-dozen or so, and an important guest star part each week...The thing that intrigues me the most about the show is that it is actually based on The Rand Corporation's projection of things to come."[41]

Director Robert Butler said Hunter was easy to work with. "He was an extremely pleasant, centered guy, and maybe decent and nice to a fault," Butler said. "But he was very amenable and very trusting...kind of a gentle guy."[42]

Gene Roddenberry's script concerned the adventures of Captain Pike and his crew on a distant planet named Talos IV. Pike answers a distress call from another Earth ship and mounts a rescue mission, only to discover that he and his crew are the pawns of an alien race that has the power to control their minds.[43]

Hunter's characterization of Captain Pike is the centerpiece of the story.

NBC executives viewed the pilot in February 1965, but rejected it as a possible series. They all agreed the story was wonderful, the acting and directing generally believable, and the special effects fine, but they felt the story might be above the heads of the average viewer at home, that it didn't have enough action and adventure, and it had too much "eroticism," including scenes of a scantily clad, green-skinned alien woman.[44]

However, NBC decided that the idea behind the series was sound, and so in March, the network asked Desilu for a second pilot. NBC asked for a number of changes in the second pilot, but a recasting of the captain was not one of them. They liked Jeffrey Hunter and told producers he could stay on.[45]

But Hunter never made it to the second pilot, which was filmed over eight days in July 1965, and which did eventually sell the series.

For various reasons, Jeff Hunter opted out; the producers of the pilot later said that Hunter liked the show but that his wife talked him out of it.[46] What the Hunters apparently were looking for was a contract similar to the one he had at Warner Bros.

"What I was given to understand," actor Leonard Nimoy said during an Archive of American Television interview in 2000, "and it may be the simple truth, was that he wanted to renegotiate...Jeffrey Hunter was a movie star, and he was concerned about his movie career, and that he asked the studio to guarantee him a feature movie role, or roles, as part of his deal for acting in this series. They were not in a position to do that, they didn't have movies to offer him. So, they couldn't make the deal, and they let it go."[47]

Star Trek at the time was being produced by Desilu, not Paramount, as it would be later. Desilu was not Warner Bros. Pictures; it was not in the motion picture business.

Publicly, Hunter said during the summer of 1965 that the timing was wrong for him to star in the second pilot. "I was asked to do it," he said. "But had I accepted, I would have been tied up much longer than I cared to be. I have several things brewing now and they should be coming to a head in the next few weeks. I love doing motion pictures and expect to be a busy as I want to be in them."[48]

It would prove to be a crucial point in Hunter's career.

Those films—*Battle Royale* from a Samuel Fuller script and *The Last Hundred Hours* from a Stanley Kubrick script—would never be made, and Hunter instead signed on board for another television pilot and a lesser film in Hong Kong called *Strange Portrait*, about a jewel thief trying to con a widow out of her fortune.[49] The film, not nearly of the stature of a Fuller or Kubrick project, was lost in a fire and never released.

Star Trek continued on without him; William Shatner took over the role of the captain (renamed James Kirk) and *Star Trek* would play on NBC for three seasons, beginning in the fall of 1966, and eventually developing a world-wide following.

What *Star Trek* would have been with Hunter in the lead role instead of Shatner is open to debate. Certainly Shatner brought his own unique characterization to the role, and his appeal in the part is one of the enduring legacies of the franchise for many of its fans.

But the character of Kirk, in the earliest episodes of the series, really isn't that much different from the character of Pike as played by Jeffrey Hunter in the first pilot. Shatner's energy came to the part later on. Where Hunter would have gone with the part is what audiences were never to discover.

Robert Butler felt that Hunter's good looks might have posed difficulties for the show. "When one is trying to bring reality into an unreal situation, that usually isn't a wise thing to do, to hire a somewhat perfect looking actor."[50]

On the other hand, director Joseph Pevney thought Hunter and *Star Trek* would have been a good fit. "He was more honest than Bill Shatner in terms of performance. Bill had a lot of tricks."[51]

The next television pilot in line for Hunter was one for a "new, one hour action-suspense-adventure-romance television series" called *Journey into Fear*.[52]

During the summer of 1965, long-time television producer William Dozier tapped suspense author Eric Ambler, who had created the *Checkmate* television series, to create a new espionage show to pitch to the networks. Hunter had guest starred on *Checkmate* in the "Waiting for Jocko" episode in 1961.

Ambler had written a famous novel under the same name, and the novel was adapted into an equally famous 1942 film, starring Joseph Cotton and Orson Welles. The novel, the film, and the new television series shared the idea of an ordinary man in an unordinary situation.

The series, though, differed from the novel and film in important ways. Ambler envisioned that the program would center on one brilliant civilian scientist, employed from time to time by a secret government group known as SPECIAL COORDINATION (SEC). Hunter signed to play the lead, Dr. Howard Graham.

Graham, as Ambler saw him, was in his early 30's, a lean, good-looking bachelor. Graham worked as a researcher at Frosch Systems, Inc. of Altadena, California when not running clandestine errands for SEC. Graham's journeys into fear consisted of undercover work all over the world, verifying and evaluating secret information that foreign agents were trying to sell to the United States, or which U.S. agents had stolen. The idea was that a scientist such as Graham was needed to make certain the intelligence material was the real thing.

The role of Graham was a good fit for Hunter and represented another chance at a series lead in a show produced by a company, Greenways, associated with a major studio, 20th Century Fox.

Ambler wrote the pilot script, and also detailed possible future episodes in his series proposal. Ambler envisioned that subsequent episodes would find Graham in all kinds of peril all over the world, including: a Russian scientist defecting to the West, Graham posing as a scientist/traitor to lure out foreign agents, the threat of chemical warfare, and an enemy agent planted in the SEC.

In Ambler's initial teleplay, "Seller's Market," Graham and a SEC agent (Sally Ann Howes) are sent to a South American country to investigate reports that a spy wants to sell German plans for a new missile guidance system to the highest bidder.[53]

Filming was done in November 1965, and went smoothly, according to Greenways executive Charles B. Fitzsimons. "Hunter was a lovely guy, an effective performer," Fitzsimons said. "He was a very nice man, gave us no problems. He was charming and handsome; his blue eyes really struck you."[54]

The production was handled by some of Hollywood's top people. The show was executive produced by Dozier through 20th Century Fox Television; produced by Ambler's wife Joan Harrison, who had produced the Alfred Hitchcock television series; and directed by Robert Stevens, a pioneer in television production and direction whose credits dated to the late 1940s. Stevens had directed episodes of both *The Twilight Zone* and *Alfred Hitchcock Presents*, and, much earlier, *Suspense*. Stevens had been the only director on the Hitchcock series to be awarded an Emmy.

There was a lot of confidence that the quality of the pilot had been high, and that the network would pick up the show for the new season. William Dozier went so far as to tell columnist Hedda Hopper in mid-January 1966 that he had *Journey Into Fear* "coming up" in September.[55]

Then the other shoe dropped: *Journey Into Fear* was not put on NBC's fall schedule.

"We were surprised," Fitzsimons said. "It was a good show, and Hunter a good performer in it. But you can never tell why networks do the things they do."[56]

Instead, NBC went with Stephanie Powers in *The Girl From Uncle, Tarzan* and, in a cruel twist of fate, *Star Trek*. Unfortunately for Hunter's fans, *Journey Into Fear* was never shown on television.

It was Hunter's third pilot in as many years, including the *Temple Houston* pilot, but not his last attempt at a network series. A few years later, when the situation comedy *The Brady Bunch* was being developed, Hunter did a screen test for the role of the father, Mike Brady, but he didn't get the part.[57]

Jeffrey Hunter's career was never quite the same after the rejection of the *Journey Into Fear* pilot in early 1966. Beset by professional disappointments, financial issues, and personal difficulties, including the end of his second marriage, the actor had no choice but to accept roles in films that were far beneath his talents.

"He had to take roles he didn't want to because they were 'B' pictures," Van Williams said. "He didn't want to star in a 'B' picture, but he had to."

This was true, for example, of *Dimension 5*, a time travel film from 1966. "It was a film you took to make a buck and stay in the business," film co-star France Nuyen said. "It was not an 'in' picture; it was an 'out.'"[58]

In 1966, Hunter signed for work in Spain in on low-budget films, including *A Witch Without a Broom* and *The Christmas Kid*.

"Europe was where the work was then," director Alvin Ganzer said. "The studios had changed. You go where the work is. A lot of people did."[59]

Subsequent film work outside of the mainstream included films such as *Find a Place to Die, Super Colt 38, Viva America* and *Sexy Susan Sins Again*, none of which were widely seen but did provide a paycheck. He also appeared in supporting roles in Hollywood films such as *Custer of the West, The Private Navy of Sgt. O'Farrell*, and *A Guide for a Married Man*.

During this same period, Hunter also kept himself in front of wider audiences with his appearances on television programs—*The Green Hornet, Daniel Boone, The Legend of Jesse James, The Monroes, The FBI, Insight*, and a two-part *Star Trek* episode that used the original series pilot as a flashback story.

However, while *The Christmas Kid, Custer of the West*, and *Find a Place to Die* were serviceable westerns, Hunter's films after 1965, taken as a whole, were a long way down from the halcyon days with John Ford.

"He just didn't get the breaks," Van Williams said.[60]

It is humbling when Hunter refers to himself as a "second-string actor," as he did in an interview published in 1969, even as he added that he had kept working because he was a "good, stable actor," one producers could depend on.[61]

In 1969, Hunter suffered two strokes, and took a bad fall at the home he was sharing with third wife Emily McLaughlin, with whom he had been happy. Emergency surgery failed. Jeffrey Hunter died on May 27, 1969. He would have turned 43 that November.

"I liked Jeff and was shocked and saddened when he died," actor James Best said.[62]

Unquestionably with Jeffrey Hunter, there is sadness in a life ended much too soon, and in the promise left unfulfilled.

What might the future have held for Hunter, had he lived? There's no reason to think he couldn't have returned to more mainstream films, along with his ongoing mainstream television work.

"Jeff Hunter was good in films, had a lot of talent," Alvin Ganzer said. "He could have made a comeback with the right script."[63]

As "Custer's conscience," Benteen,
in *Custer of the West.*
(Milton T. Moore Photos)

"A very decent man," director Joseph Pevney, who directed Hunter twice, first in *The Equitable Life Theatre* pilot and then in a 1966 episode of *The Legend of Jesse James*, said. "He knew his stuff. Producers liked him. Directors liked him. A solid performer."[64]

"He was terribly handsome," France Nuyen said. "Very pleasant, courteous and professional. He went out of his way to be courteous and he took special care to be polite."[65]

Those on the set of *Temple Houston* in 1963 and 1964 also remembered his kindness. Actress Julie Parrish, who appeared in the episode "The Guardian," said, "I played his ward in that episode and was an angry kid out to avenge my father's death... I was shooting at people and as my ward he gave me a public spanking. I remember he had a sense of humor about that. We laughed about it, and I remember when another actor was too rough with me in a fight scene, Mr. Hunter objected to that."[66]

There is an element of humanity that runs through Hunter's best work, what the actor described as the brotherhood message of *King of Kings*. It's also found in characters he played in other films, such as in *The Searchers*, when Martin Pawley defends Debbie against the racist Ethan Edwards; in *No Man is an Island*, when George Tweed is bothered by the racism he encounters among his rescuers; and in *Sergeant Rutledge*, when Lt. Cantrell defends Rutledge, a black man accused of murder. The quality is also evident in Hunter's television work, such as in *Death Valley Days*, when Dr. Walter Reed protects his young patient from soldiers and Indians alike; and in his appearance on *Combat*, when his character, Sgt. Dane, the priest turned soldier, is guilt-ridden about the killing he'd done. It's clearly evident in *Temple Houston*, as well, when Houston defends those clients who need defending, in the name of the law and justice.

Robert Douglas, who directed Hunter in the 1967 episode of the television western series *The Monroes*, echoed others when he said Hunter "was a delightful young actor to work with, co-operative and talented."[67]

That's the Jeffrey Hunter fans still remember—the talented and likeable actor who was Jesus in *King of Kings*; the astonishingly handsome star who smiles at Constance Towers as the music comes up at the end of *Sergeant Rutledge*; and the actor who came across so well on television, be it as the troubled 'soiled priest' in a the 1962 "Lost Sheep, Lost Shepard" episode of *Combat*, as the heroic captain in *Star Trek*, or as *Temple Houston* in those twenty-six episodes in 1963 and 1964.

"I had a lot of respect for him as an actor and as a person," Van Williams said. "He was one of the nicest guys I ever met. Things didn't go right for him, and they should have, because if anybody deserved to be a big, big star, it was Jeffrey Hunter."[68]

§

ENDNOTES

1. Takei, interview
2. Williams, interview.
3. Jeffrey Hunter biography, NBC- TV, Warner Bros. Archive, University of Southern California, Los Angeles.
4. "Ten Push-Ups and I Simmer Down," page 26
5. Williams, interview.
6. Terry, page F 13.
7. Parsons, October 1, 1961.

8. Jeffrey Hunter letter to John Ford, August 3, 1960, John Ford Papers, Lilly Library, Indiana University, Bloomington, Indiana.

9. Parsons, October 1, 1961

10. Takei, interview.

11. "Suzie" was written by Terence Maples from a story by Virgil C. Gerlach, and directed by Bud Townsend.

12. Nunn, pages. 40- 41.

13. Ibid, page 41

14. MGM publicity materials, *King of Kings*

15. Parsons, October 1, 1961.

16. "Big Picture-Maker Samuel Bronston Based in Dallas for Comeback Drive," pages 31-32

17. Jeffrey Hunter letter to John Ford, August 3, 1960, John Ford Papers, Lilly Library, Indiana University, Bloomington, Indiana.

18. Nunn, page 41

19. Williams, interview

20. "$ign of the Cross," page 55

21. Walsh, page 74

22. Crowther, 41: 2

23. Landry, page 6

24. Hartung, page 152- 153

25. Ibid, page 152

26. "Everybody a Bible Student: Liked the Book Better than the Pic," pages 5, 24

27. Arneel, pages 3, 21

28. "Big Picture-Maker Samuel Bronston Based in Dallas for Comeback Drive," pages 31-32

29. Ibid

30. Thomas, "Hollywood," page 14

31. Johnson, page 5

32. Williams, interview

33. Ganzer, interview

34. One example is Hank Grant's article "Jeff Hunter Breaks Hollywood Jinx" in 1963.

35. Scheurer, page C 11

36. Pruess, page 29

37. "Jeff Hunter Defied 'Jinx' in Film Role," *TV Roundup, Chicago's Sunday American*, May 31–June 6, 1964.

38. Pruess, page 29

39. Hefferman, page 18

40. Solow, page 36- 37

41. Schmitt, January 30, 1965.
42. Asherman, page 95
43. "The Cage," available through Paramount Home Video
44. Solow, page 59
45. Ibid, page 60
46. Ibid, page 63
47. Leonard Nimoy, Archive of American Television interview
48. Spiro, "Happy in Hollywood," page 4
49. Stone, e-mail
50. Asherman, page 95
51. Pevney, interview
52. *Journey Into Fear*, Eric Ambler Collection, Howard Gotlieb Archival Research Center, Boston University, Boston, MA
53. Ibid
54. Fitzsimons, interview
55. Hopper, "Foy Will Film 'Seeds of Madrid,'" page C 10
56. Fitzsimons, interview
57. Schwartz, page 100
58. Nuyen, interview
59. Ganzer, interview
60. Williams, interview
61. Hoffman, June 1969
62. Best, e-mail
63. Ganzer, interview
64. Pevney, interview
65. Nuyen, interview
66. Parrish, e-mail
67. Douglas, letter
68. Williams, interview

Chapter Five
Jack Elam as George Taggart

By most accounts, Jack Elam was a legendary card player.

"Jack was a whiz at cards," actor James Best, who co-starred with Elam in episodes of *Temple Houston* and again in the film *Firecreek*, which starred Henry Fonda and James Stewart, said. "*Firecreek* was a great example. He took all of Hank's money in a card game."[1]

Director Burt Kennedy, who cast Elam in several of the pictures he directed, wrote, "Most players just hand their money over to him when they sit down to play poker with him…it saves time."[2]

Kennedy called Elam a dear friend. "A man with a face only a mother and millions of western fans could love." [3]

"Being a contract player at Warner Brothers, one of the good things was that they used a lot of good people," Van Williams said. "Jack Elam did a lot of shows at Warner Brothers and I was there for six years and I did a lot of shows with him. He was one hell of a nice guy and one hell of an actor."[4]

Elam brought his sense of humor to the back lot at Warner Bros. for the filming of the *Temple Houston* series.

In the episode "The Law and Big Annie," Marshal Taggart inherits a four-ton elephant, and Elam trained for hours with the elephant, named Sheeba. Elam and Sheeba reportedly developed quite a friendship during these training sessions, and eventually Sheeba would place her trunk on Elam's head while the actor fed her peanuts. On Elam's command, Sheeba would kneel, stand, and even follow him on the lot's western streets. When a studio executive visited the set, Elam approached him with Sheeba alongside, and said, "Now about that new dressing room…"[5]

The casting of Jack Elam as the U.S. Deputy Marshal George Taggart would prove to be one of the best decisions the producers of *Temple Houston* made. His characterization of the gunslinger and sometimes lawman drew upon his career as a film and TV 'heavy,' and added a great deal of realism to the *Temple Houston* series.

Taggart was a lawman who hired himself out to the various communities in the Southwest in need of some temporary law enforcement.

Jack Elam as George Taggart, with player.
(Western TV Photos)

"I don't play the part like a lawman, though," Elam said. "In some of the shows I'm marshal when the episode begins and in others I get the job at the end. But I have no message in the world as the marshal."[6]

In the series prospectus, Taggart was described as a man out of step with his world, with a look of villainy that frightened some people and partly explained the distance he kept between himself and a lot of people. Taggart was fascinating, though, because of his sense of right and wrong—a sense that was flexible, depending upon the moment and the mood and the need.

Taggart was well known throughout the territory as a fast gun and a very capable gunfighter and lawman. He had a reputation of being fearless and someone you didn't cross; George Taggart was someone you wanted on your side.[7]

George Taggart and Houston were played as friendly enemies, even as antagonists. In the episode "The Guardian," Taggart fires warning shots at Houston as the attorney approaches on horseback; in "The Twisted Rope," the two have a no-holds barred fist fight.

"I never think about the badge until somebody asks me about it," Elam said of his Taggart role. "As far as I'm concerned, I'm still the heavy and I'll always be the heavy."[8]

There were those who said Elam stole the show from Hunter. "The co-star is the marshal, played by Jack Elam," Rick DuBrow wrote in January 1964. "A fine villain type who keeps getting thrown into series with blank-faced stars, and carrying them."[9]

If indeed one believes that Elam was a scene-stealer in the series, it would not be the first— or the last—time. Burt Kennedy recounted how "I wanted to cast Jack in *The Train Robbers*, opposite (John) Wayne and Ann-Margaret. Wayne balked at this because, in *Rio Lobo*, Jack stole the picture away from him, or so the critics claimed." [10]

In most of his early film and television appearances—and by the time he was cast in *Temple Houston*, Elam had appeared in more than fifty films (including 1952's *Lure of the Wilderness* with Jeff Hunter) and on more than one hundred episodes of television shows—Elam played the villain.

"Jack looked lean and mean in those days," Burt Kennedy wrote. "He was cast as the bad guy for years."[11]

A 1963 *TV Guide* profile described Elam this way: "He has the look of classic villains: a slack, loose-lipped, too-large mouth; discolored, uneven teeth which should be brought to the attention of the American Dental Association; a bumpy nose; bulbous, protruding eyes; and a head of hair that is both jet black and receding."[12]

"I was never a hero in western movies," Elam said on one occasion. "Nice guys, sometimes, but no heroes. I made 24 appearances on *Gunsmoke*. The first ten years I was the heavy. Then I got a director who didn't see me as a heavy. He'd have me as an old friend of Matt Dillon's who would ride into town."[13]

Temple Houston was not the first time Elam played the good guy; he also played a deputy marshal in the 1963 Warner Bros. series *The Dakotas*. Jules Schermer, the producer of that series, said, "I've always considered him one of the best actors in the business."[14]

The Dakotas premiered in January 1963 and depicted the adventures of a U.S. marshal and his three deputies in the Black Hills and Badlands of the Dakota Territory. Elam played J.D. Smith, an ex-gunslinger.

"I'm ashamed to be seen wearing a badge," Elam said of his part. "I kind of hide it under my vest. And every time I have to bad mouth the heavies, the words stick in my throat."[15]

"One look at him and the character of J.D. Smith was born," Schermer said. "A realist, a cynic, a gunslinger who had been paid to get the marshal but decided he liked the marshal's case better, so joined forces with him."[16]

"The public may not accept seeing me not get killed," Elam said just before the premiere of *The Dakotas*. "Western fans are annoyed by the unexpected, and it's out of character with me to live to the end of the episode."[17]

Jack Elam was born November 13, 1920 in Miami, Arizona, and grew up in Phoenix. His mother died when he was born. His father was nearly blind, and that impairment led to Elam's first experience with accounting. His father worked as a property manager for a building and loan company, but needed his eleven-year-old son to do the math for him.

An eye injury incurred while a Boy Scout gave Elam one of his trademarks—the loss of sight in his left eye. He and his father moved to Turlock, California, when Elam was 16. Feeling somewhat restless, Elam moved and by the time he was 17 he was married and working for Standard Oil as an auditor. That first marriage lasted 23 years, until his wife died in 1958. He remarried in 1961.

Elam was educated in business at junior colleges in Santa Monica and Modesto.

"Jack started in the picture business as an accountant," Burt Kennedy wrote. "He was also the night manager of the Beverly Hills Hotel, and a prime mover in the building of the famous Bel-Air Hotel." [18]

In fact, Elam's jobs prior to his switch to acting were all rooted in business. He was a division auditor for Standard Oil, assistant auditor for the Beverly Hills Hotel, auditor and manager of the Bel-Air Hotel, special tax consultant for Samuel Goldwyn, and a $500/week motion picture auditor.

"I loved accounting," Elam said. "I think I had more self-respect as an auditor than as an actor.

"If I'd go before a board of directors with a balance sheet, they'd have to accept whatever I had submitted because they didn't know any different. I got respect. As an actor, maybe some people like what I do and others don't."[19]

As an accountant, Elam developed a budget system for independent motion picture production, but he turned to acting in the late 1940s. Part of the reason was that his one good eye was starting to give out under the strain of all the financial work, but Elam cited another reason, as well.

"I kept seeing these actors' paychecks going across my desk," he said. "All that money, and these characters were coming in late and not working when they got in. I figured that was the racket for me."[20]

Elam's lack of experience didn't deter him. "You might say I talked my way in," he said. "As an auditor, I knew where the money was, I knew the right guys at the right banks.

"So this producer, Dick Templeton, needed dough for a picture he wanted to make, something called *Trailin' West*...So I said, 'Dick, you give me a part, I'll get you the money.' We both got what we wanted."[21]

There was always work after that.

"My first real break was on a picture called *Rawhide* in 1951, with Tyrone Power and Susan Hayward, for Twentieth Century Fox," Elam said. "I was put under contract with Fox for seven years. Which lasted one year. They didn't give me anything to do, and so I begged out of it."[22]

Elam and Power became friends, and Elam credited Power with helping him learn about filmmaking and getting his career off the ground.

Elam never looked back. His career would come to encompass dozens of films and appearances in television series.

"There were years I thought I was a leading man," he said. "Only the reviews convinced me otherwise. The only thing I secretly pine for is steady employment. I try to live as high off the hog as I can. My idea of poverty is a hotel room with only one bathroom."[23]

Elam was known as an asset to any production he was involved in, be it a two-day shoot, as he did on *High Noon*, or a longer role, as he did on television in *Temple Houston*. Wherever he worked and whomever he played, Jack Elam could be counted on as a pro.

"He was a character of the first water," James Best said. "A fine actor and one hell of a nice guy."[24]

Elam's approach to acting was straightforward. "I live by and believe in just one thing. Honesty. If I believe in a role, the audience will believe in it. I have to have fun with a role, have to enjoy myself. I don't believe in all this method stuff."[25]

As *The BFI Companion to the Western* pointed out, "Invariably playing character roles, which were on occasion sadistic, his mere presence was enough to establish evil intent."[26]

Asked by a reporter in 1979 if he had enjoyed playing villains, Elam said, "I like to work. I didn't have any choice. I've turned down roles, but not many. Mostly because the roles weren't big enough. Some for content. I used to have a dollar sign printed on my script cover and on my chair.

"Not to imply that I'm a money hungry actor, but to remind me I'm a professional actor. I don't know anything about art, but in thirty years I've never been late. It's a job, I punch a clock because I get paid."[27]

Elam's many Western films included *Trailin' West* and *The Sundowners* (1949); *High Lonesome* (1950); *Ride, Vaquero!* (1952); *Cattle Queen of Montana*, *Vera Cruz*, and *The Far Country* (1954); *The Man From Laramie*, *Wichita*, and *Man Without a Star* (1955); *Gunfight at the OK Corral* (1956); *The Commancheros* (1961), and *Firecreek* (1968).

Firecreek, the Fonda–Stewart picture, was typical of Elam's appearances in film. He said he knew without even reading the script that his character would be killed off. "In six previous films with Jimmy, I've been shot by him four times, killed by a knife once and on the other occasion trampled to death by his horse," Elam said. "The only question was how and when I'd be done in."[28]

The Hollywood heavy began to change in the 1960s and 1970s, not always to Elam's liking. As he told *The Los Angeles Times* in 1977, "The heavy today is not usually my kind of guy.

"In the old days, Rory Calhoun was the hero because he was the hero and I was the heavy because I was the heavy, and nobody cared what my problem was. And I didn't either. I robbed the bank because I wanted the money.

"I've played all kinds of weirdos but I've never done the quiet, sick type. I never had a problem, other than the fact I was just bad."[29]

On television, Elam appeared as a guest star on *Tales of Wells Fargo, Zorro, The Texan, The Rifleman, Bronco, Lawman, The Restless Gun, Cheyenne, Gunsmoke*, and *Bonanza*, among many others.

Elam was a regular in *The Dakotas* (1963), *Temple Houston* (1963–64), *The Texas Wheelers* (1974), *Struck by Lightning* (1979), *Detective in the House* (1985), and *Easy Street* (1986). He enjoyed his work as a regular player on television.

In *The Texas Wheelers*, Elam played Zack Wheeler, a man who returns home after eight months away, hunting for gold. Wheeler finds himself in charge of four motherless children. "It's a piece of various roles. He's a nice guy, but he's a jerk. He's a lazy loudmouth with a good heart."[30]

In the 1979 series *Struck By Lightning*, he played Frank, the caretaker of an old New England Inn. Ted Stein inherited the inn in the series. Frank and Stein were the main characters, in other words. "I've never done horror before but I've been in some horrible films," Elam said about the situation comedy.[31]

The turn to comedy in Elam's career came in 1969 when Burt Kennedy broke the string of villainess roles by casting Elam in a light-hearted role.

"He was so identified with being a heavy that United Artists thought I was crazy when I wanted him for the comic deputy in *Support Your Local Sheriff*," Kennedy wrote. "I knew Jack was a riot personally and that he'd be great. He was, and it started a whole new career for him."[32]

The two friends also worked together in *Support Your Local Gunfighter*. "Jack was so funny in that," Kennedy recalled, "I had a hard time casting him in a straight role from then on."[33]

Elam also gave some credit to the Walt Disney Company for the chance to play something other than the bad guy.

"Blame that on the Disney Studios," Elam said. "Old Walt said he never believed it when I'd pistol whip Maureen O' Hara or someone like that. Old Walt said anybody with my puss just had to be a comic and I'd been dying to do those roles for a long time."[34]

Elam first worked for Disney in 1968's *Never a Dull Moment*, then in 1969's *Ride a Northbound Horse* on television, and again with a part in 1970's *The Wild Country*.

Two of Elam's television appearances in the 1970s demonstrate his remarkable versatility and his gifts as an actor.

On December 27, 1971, Elam appeared on the "P.S. Murry Christmas" episode of *Gunsmoke* on CBS as Titus Spangler, a handyman at an orphanage run by cranky spinster Emma Grundy (Jeannette Nolan). At Christmas time, Grundy is determined that the orphans not get their hopes up, lest they be disappointed. Just as determined, Spangler springs a group of the children from the orphanage and lands with them in Dodge City, hoping to show them the true meaning of Christmas. As Spangler, Elam is warm, generous, and funny, as he shows not only the children, but also Ms. Grundy, what it is they've been missing. It is a fine turn by the veteran character actor.[35]

Six years later, Elam appeared in two 1977 episodes of the ABC-TV miniseries *How the West Was Won*, again directed by Burt Kennedy. He played Cully Madigan, a mountain man on a murderous rampage against the Indians who have kidnapped his son. The Army believes that Madigan's rage threatens to create a new Indian uprising. Tracked down by fellow mountain man Zeb Macahan (James Arness), Madigan says that he doesn't want to trigger an uprising; all he wants is his boy back.

Elam's character is strong, independent, vengeful, frightening, softhearted, and wistful. Madigan longs for the old days, before the encroachment of civilization on the West, and he lived by the code of the mountain men. Madigan's death—he is killed by a bullet from Macahan before Indians peel his skin off at a fiery stake—is a shattering and memorable moment of episodic television.[36]

Burt Kennedy wrote lovingly of his friend in his book, *Hollywood Trail Boss*, calling Elam "a world class actor."[37]

Indeed.

Jack Elam was inducted into the Hall of Great Western Performers at the National Cowboy and Western Heritage Museum in 1994. He died on October 20, 2003.

§

ENDNOTES

1. Best, e-mail
2. Kennedy, page 33.
3. Ibid
4. Williams, interview.
5. "Big Scale Friendship Seen on 'Temple Houston' Lot," page 16.
6. Finnigan, "Ex- Heavy Jack Elam Most Unusual Marshal," page 7 G.

7. *Temple Houston* Series Prospectus, Warner Bros. Archive, University of Southern California, Los Angeles.

8. Finnigan, "Ex-Heavy Jack Elam Most Unusual Marshal," page 7 G.

9. DuBrow, "Houston Falls Flat," page 40.

10. Kennedy, page 36.

11. Ibid, page 33

12. "The Picture of a Classic Villain," page 16

13. Buck, "Jack Elam: Monstrously Fun," page 6 C

14. "The Picture of a Classic Villain," page 16

15. Finnigan, "Ex-Heavy Jack Elam Most Unusual Marshal," page 7 G.

16. "The Picture of a Classic Villain," page 16

17. West, page 5

18. Kennedy, page 33

19. Shull, page P 13

20. "The Picture of a Classic Villain," page 16

21. Ibid

22. Kennedy, page 35

23. Stewart, page B 4

24. Best, e-mail

25. "The Picture of a Classic Villain," page 17

26. Buscombe, page 339

27. Buck, "Jack Elam: Monstrously Fun," page 6 C

28. "Elam Killed Again by Jimmy Stewart," page 2

29. Calhoun, page) 31.

30. Buck, "Jack Elam's Image has Changed," page 29

31. Buck, "Jack Elam: Monstrously Fun," page 6 C

32. Kennedy, page 34

33. Ibid, page 34

34. Bawden, page 10

35. The episode was written by William Kelley and directed by Herb Wallenstein.

36. The writers credited on the miniseries were Ron Bishop, John Mantley, Jim Byrnes, William Kelley, and Earl W. Wallace.

37. Kennedy, page 33

Chapter Six
Good Stories

Jack Elam remembered *Temple Houston* as having good stories.[1] It is evident that the researchers and writing staff at Warner Brothers worked very hard, despite the time crunch, to find new and different story ideas, and to try to create something different.

Temple Houston was not the first television western to feature a lawyer as a lead character—not nearly. *Black Saddle*, which featured a main character as an attorney; *Sugarfoot*, with its title character a law correspondence student; and Disney's *The Nine Lives of Elfego Baca*, about a frontier lawyer battling injustice, had all come before. *Temple Houston* was unique, however, in that it was the first hour-long series to really combine, as the major part of its format, the legal drama and the Western.

The hope was that *Temple Houston* could combine the best aspects of both genres, tap into the strengths of each, while avoiding the clichés. The story of the establishment of law and order in the West was a compelling one, as first marshals and then judges and lawyers worked to overcome the resistance they encountered in settlements built during the western expansion.

Again—by the time *Temple Houston* premiered in 1963, the Western had been a major staple of the network schedules for years. The same was true of the legal drama. In its legal components and themes, *Temple Houston* was following in a long line of television shows about the legal system. *Perry Mason* was certainly the most popular, and most important, in terms of its influence on the legal genre.

Other courtroom dramas on television up to 1963 included *The Defenders*, *Sam Benedict*, *Mr. District Attorney*, *The Law and Mr. Jones*, *Lockup*, and *Court of Last Resort*.

There had been enough legal dramas seen by the viewing public that by the time *Temple Houston* aired in 1963–64, a debate was ongoing between television producers and members of the legal community as to what impact, if any, these programs were having on the public's knowledge of the legal system and its opinion of that system.

Examples of both sides of the conversation were presented in the journal *Television Quarterly* in the fall of 1964. Attorney Edward Bennett Williams roundly criticized the legal drama: "I cringe and am sickened by the slick, glib legerdemain of television's lawyers. Our system of justice simply does not work that way…

"Television's dramatists, while observing technical details, leave an impression that the scholarship of law is a bore; a bore that is unnecessary to successful practice.

"Students have come to understand that criminal cases are decided by rhetoric; that the outcome depends on malevolent tricks; that the lawyer is always the key factor in winning and losing."[2]

Reginald Rose, the creator and executive producer of *The Defenders* on CBS, countered with: "If what results is a fuller understanding of the meaning of law and justice among multitudes of human beings, then the charge of 'unrealistic' is pointless."[3]

Of course, one of the hopes of the producers of *Temple Houston* was that the series could use legal cases from Houston's life and the years in which he lived to build episodes around. The stories could provide insight into differences in legal matters between then and the current day. Viewers encountered both sides of the argument as presented by Edward Bennett Williams and Reginald Rose.

The real-life Temple Houston was determined to step out of his famous father's shadow, to use his skill as an attorney to bring law and order to the American Southwest. *Temple Houston* as seen on NBC, in both its serious and more lighthearted formats, attempted to tap into this historical truth through its (admittedly) fictional narratives.

The trend was set in the very first episode, "The Twisted Rope." As Houston tries to defend the half-brothers of Dorrie Chevenix, who have been charged with murder in the death of a lawman, he must move fast to prove his clients innocent before lynch mob fever takes over. What follows would appear on the surface to be typical television legal drama theatrics, as the story plays out in court. There is a visit to the crime scene and Houston's reconstruction of the incident, a surprise witness, and Houston's legal savvy that secures a confession from that witness.[4]

But as Francis Nevins pointed out in *Prime Time Law*, there was more to the story than that. Early in the episode, Houston tells Taggart that there was more to justice than getting caught and getting hung; it also meant a fair trial, with counsel. As Nevins said, "These lines, written less than five months after the Supreme Court's landmark decision in *Gideon v. Wainwright*, furnish a superb illustration of how real-world jurisprudence impacts on the popular culture."[5]

Gideon v. Wainwright was the decision by the U.S. Supreme Court that said that state courts were required, under the Constitution, to provide legal counsel in criminal cases to those defendants who could not afford one.

Nevins also believed that there was added realism given the story by the fact that Houston defended his clients as vigorously as he did. While they were innocent of the crime they were charged with, they were guilty of abusing their own half-sister Dorrie over the years. Houston must break Dorrie on the stand through a series of increasingly harsh, pointed questions. He feels for her situation, but is duty-bound to get at the truth, that it was Dorrie's bullet that killed the marshal on the street, not the bullets belonging to her brothers. Houston makes it clear to Taggart that while he won the case for his clients, he didn't have to be happy about it.[6]

Hunter as the famed frontier lawyer. *(Photofest)*

Houston makes a further stand for a fair trial for his clients when he tells Taggart that the brothers deserved protection from the law before, during, and after the trial.[7]

In the series' eighth episode, "Jubilee," we see just how much Houston believes in the rule of law, and what it means on the frontier, as he decides to defend a man accused of killing one of his friends. Houston's commitment to the "Letter of the Law" is also clearly demonstrated in the third episode of the series, as he faces a test of his legal ethics as he defends three clients, one of whom he believes to be guilty of the charges they all face.[8]

On television, Temple Houston was clearly portrayed as one of those who helped build the legal system in the American Southwest, by not only demonstrating through the practice of law that legal battles counted for as much as gun battles, but also by demonstrating that the establishment of the legal system meant the coming of a more civilized society.

In E.M. Parsons' story, "Gallows at Galilee," the series combined a composite historical character with an examination of what was and was not justice—in the old west and the current day.

In the episode, Houston argues with Taggart over the methods being used by Judge Galen Stark, a so-called 'hanging judge.' Taggart wonders what it is that Stark has done that is so wrong; the marshal argues that the judge is a lawman, just as he is, but he uses a rope instead of a gun.

Houston tells Taggart that Stark uses the law to create injustice. Later, Houston tells his client, a young man accused of murder, that all is not lost because they still had their appearance in court in front of them, inferring to him that justice was still possible through the sanctuary of the courtroom.

Still later, as Houston and Taggart continue to investigate the murder case, Houston wonders out loud about what he calls Judge Stark's treatment of capital cases; Houston says it is not ordinary.

Taggart maintains the judge is trying to make people respect and obey the law, but Houston doesn't believe that hanging everyone is the way to do it. Taggart says the law is where he points his gun and his badge, but Houston argues that idea is overly dependent on fear, fear with a capital letter.[9]

Houston's skill as an attorney was often all that stood between order and chaos. His legal acumen helped set straight the scales of justice.

In "Toll the Bell Slowly," written by Robert Leslie Bellem and Carey Wilbur from a story by Wilbur, Houston again demonstrates his passion for the law and justice, and his willingness to fight for his clients, when he and Taggart rides miles and miles to reach Forbesville in search of a potential witness in the case of a client Houston is defending. Upon their arrival, however, Houston and Taggart discover that Charlie Bailey is scheduled to hang in just a few hours for the murder of a leading citizen of the town.

Houston argues for a two-week delay in the hanging when he discovers that Bailey can indeed clear his client with testimony. The town is not willing to delay the hanging, however, and the Houston faces a race against time to prove Bailey innocent of the murder charge and discover the truth. The frontier attorney is willing to go up against the Forbes family, the town's namesakes, in his search for the truth to clear Bailey.

In a confrontation with town founder Daniel Forbes, Houston says he sympathizes with Forbes over the loss of his son, the murdered man, but says he cannot drop the matter because of his client, a man sitting on death row for a murder he did not commit. Charles Bailey is his client's only alibi, and Houston will not give up the fight. He even tries to delay the hanging with a legal maneuver—asking Taggart to take a last minute written deposition from the condemned man. In the end, Houston clears Bailey, saving his life, and, one assumes, the life of his other client once testimony is provided. [10]

Houston's failed attempt to delay the hanging in "Toll the Bell Slowly" to give him more time to investigate on behalf of the condemned man was not the only time in the series Houston was seen to use any and all means on behalf of his clients. In true network television, defense attorney style, Houston would even break the law if it meant securing information vital to his client's case.

In the episode "The Dark Madonna," for instance, Houston resorts to breaking and entering not just once, but twice, in search of clues to clear his client, Juan Ortega, who's been accused in the killing of a local man who was shot in the back. With Taggart away escorting a prisoner, Houston is left alone to discover the truth.

The case against Houston's client is built on what the local sheriff describes as good and sufficient evidence—Ortega had been seen arguing with the dead man, and his gun was found near the body. Houston, on the other hand, must build his defense case from the bottom up. His successful courtroom defense of Ortega is predicated upon his ability to motivate the jury and judge to see his client's side, despite the wave of community resentment against both Houston and the accused.[11]

Later in the series, Houston would use his legal skills to simply outwit his antagonists in a given episode, often outside of court. In "The Town That Trespassed," for example, Houston must stop a takeover of the town of Lindley by Charity Simpson and her attorney, Martin Purcell, who have a legal deed to all of the land the town was built on. The couple is trying to blackmail the town into making a large payment to purchase the deed. Houston breaks up the scheme by presenting the new "owners" with the tax bill paid annually by the town—$5,212, due immediately. The couple decides to accept a much smaller cash payment of $1,600 from the town to buy the deed.[12]

The episode, one of the last of the series, featured yet another version of the femme fatale—in this case, Charity Simpson, who is innocently looking for a payday. The series had also featured female con artists in "Ten Rounds for Baby" and "Fracas at Kiowa Flats."

Houston also used a bit of legal chicanery to save the day in "The Guardian," the episode in which he serves as a ward for orphaned children who find themselves in the middle of a property line and watering hole dispute.

The cattle belonging to Houston and the orphans need water, but the watering hole on their side of the disputed property line is dry and the one on the other side is full of water. Marshal Taggart is guarding the fenced property line to keep the two sides from shooting at each other, and Houston promises Taggart that he will not cross the fence. Instead, Houston simply moves the fence, reminding Taggart that he promised not to cross the fence, but said nothing about the property line. The cattle have plenty of water, and Houston tells the other rancher that he'll need a court order to stop the cattle from drinking.[13]

The shift in the tone of the series, starting with episode number twelve, "Fracas at Kiowa Flats," had created an entirely different narrative approach. There grew to be less courtroom drama than originally conceived.

At the beginning, Jack Webb had said that scripts would be based on actual legal cases in the post-Civil War period. This would add to the color and authenticity of the series, and allow for the full development of the Temple Houston character, taking full advantage of the real Houston's career as an attorney as the basis for stories.

But the emphasis on Houston the attorney changed with the tweaks to the format. As *The New York Times* reported, "*Temple Houston* was originally going to observe all the rules of courtroom gamesmanship on the Old Frontier...Temple decided to give up the bar and move to the range. The son of Sam Houston is only occasionally heard saying, 'Gentlemen of the Jury'..." [14]

The change meant that while Houston was often seen gathering facts and evidence, he was seen in the courtroom less often. In episodes such as "Enough Rope," broadcast on December 19, 1963, and "The Town That Trespassed," broadcast on March 26, 1964, Houston is referred to as an attorney, but performs almost no legal work.

The shift in tone of the series was dramatic; whereas in an earlier episode such as "Gallows in Galilee," the issue of a judge potentially abusing his position was treated as a potential affront to society, in "Enough Rope," the depiction of a public official, the mayor of Lindley, Texas, cooking the town accounting books and openly offering residents bribes leading up to an election is played mostly with humor. [15]

Certainly, "Fracas at Kiowa Flats" was sending the series in an entirely new direction. Written by Carey Wilbur, the episode had no court case for Houston, only a mystery or two to solve. Riding a stagecoach with other passengers from Tascosa to Appaloosa, Houston's immediate task is two-fold: to convince a postal official that the mail contract should stay in the hands of Concho Charlie, who runs the stage line; and, upon reaching his destination, defend Bill Gotch on a horse stealing charge. Gotch had been apprehended by Taggart and is now being escorted by Houston to trial. The stage runs heads on into a long running feud between two Civil War veterans, who are firing at each other at Kiowa Flats. The stage cannot proceed. As background to this situation, there is one other story line—Houston agreeing to help a beautiful visitor to Tascosa find her long-lost family. In the end, Houston ends the feud, exposes the woman as a fraud, and saves the mail contract.

In Jack Turley's "The Town That Trespassed," Houston must find a way to thwart off a con man and his fiancée, who have a legal deed to the property that the town of Lindley sits on. Houston sends a wire off for information, and wines and dines the unsuspecting fiancée, all as a means of gathering information he needs, but the case is not settled in court, and there were no futures hanging in the balance as a jury decided the fate of those involved.

In "Ten Rounds for Baby," broadcast on January 30, 1964, Houston is referred to as "counselor" quite often in the story of a local man who climbs into a boxing ring to win over his fiancé's two brothers. But here again, Houston's vocation as an attorney serves him in the role of town father, not practicing attorney. The courtroom is never seen and never referred to; there is no legal case. Houston uses his analytical skills to smoke out the con being perpetrated on the town by some of those involved in the boxing match.

"Enough Rope," written by Robert Vincent Wright, featured an election between the corrupt mayor of Lindley and his opponent, Temple Houston, who decided to throw his hat into the ring just days before the polls opened. Houston's strategy: do nothing but play a game of chess in the mayor's own saloon, make him nervous enough to make a mistake, and catch him in the act. Houston and Taggart capture one of the mayor's henchmen in the act of cooking the town's books, enough to force the mayor to resign. It's not enough to get Houston elected mayor, however; he informs the town that he is still considered an official resident of a different county. Conveniently, however, Houston has cast a write-in vote for an unannounced candidate, the former

"The Case for William Gotch," one of the episodes with a lighter tone, with Hunter and guest star Erin O'Donnell. *(Photofest)*

mayor, who is therefore put back into office with one vote.[16]

Here again, Houston is seen as clever, and a step ahead of the criminal element, but it is more as a guiding force for the community rather than as a crusading attorney.

With both the western genre and the legal drama to draw from, the series had a unique opportunity to tell stories about a wide-range of topics, be it under the more serious approach the series started with, or the lighter approach it ended with.

For example, the episode written by Ron Bishop, "Do Onto Others, Then Gallop," broadcast on March 19, 1964, was as much about community as it was about the mystery. As Richard M. Merlman wrote, "...the hero, Houston, is accused unjustly of a murder he was forced to commit in self-defense. The murder is a frame-up intended to discredit Houston in the eyes of his fellow citizens. The outside villains succeed in casting suspicion on him, but finally Houston exposes them.

"Most often these attacks come from thieves and other lawless roving bands whose major motivation is either money or blind hostility to community life." [17]

"Ten Rounds for Baby," written by William R. Cox, is another episode that looks at the value of community, though the outside forces in this story did not come to town bearing arms or weapons of any kind, really. But the threat from outside was just as real as any bank robber—when Kate Fitzpatrick (Anne Francis) steps off the stagecoach, she is there to dupe Houston, Taggart, and the entire town of Lindley. She's one of the masterminds behind a con that involves bets being placed on a rigged boxing match, and means to make off with the money. Houston, as the hero, must defend his community, and set things right, by investigating his suspicions and exposing the con. [18]

In exposing these villains and their true motives, Houston demonstrates the value of community life, and the need to fight off those outside forces attacking that community.

Other staples of the Western story were the subjects of other episodes. Water and property rights were the backdrop to "The Guardian," in which Houston is appointed ward of two children, one a rebellious teenage girl, whose father has been killed in a dispute over a watering hole and a property line; squatter rights were the subject of "The Siege at Thayer's Bluff," in which Houston takes on the case of a couple living on land claimed by a rancher; a land squabble, as seen in episode number eleven, "Seventy Times Seven," in which Houston uses some legal sleight-of-hand to protect peaceful farmers when he gets a court order naming Marshal Taggart as the family's defender; and the innocent man sentenced to hang, in "Toll the Bell Slowly."[19]

One thing that didn't change, no matter what half of the season, was that writers looked to history for story ideas.

In real life, Temple Houston was renowned for his courtroom skills as an attorney, whether he was prosecuting the accused or defending them. In this series there was ample opportunity to see the fictional Houston use oratory in the manner of the real-life man he was based on.

Warren Douglas' story "Sam's Boy" concerned three old-timers who travel to Lindley looking to enlist the services of Sam Houston's son in their cause—creating a second Republic of Texas, with Temple Houston as its first president. Sam's boy, they say again, will be the first President of the Second Grand Republic of Texas!

Houston tells the men over dinner that the idea is impossible, ridiculous, and even treasonable.

The three men—86-year-old Doc Webb, who rode with Sam Houston; 86-year-old Henry Hicks, who also rode with Sam Houston; and 87-year-old Billy Rogers—argue that the Texas State Constitution was set up to give citizens the right to divide into five states. Doc Webb tells Houston that when Texas joined the Union Sam Houston and others weren't always certain they were doing the right thing. Webb says the door was left open a crack just in case they ever decided that a change was needed.

Houston tries to reason with Webb, and tells him the law is obsolete, and he doesn't think it ever applied to seceding from the Union, anyway, and that the people of Texas would tear them to pieces if they started something like that.

Webb, Rogers, and Hicks say they want to set up the new republic to honor Sam Houston, and to give the Cherokee a decent place to live, side by side with any Texan who wanted to join them.

Eventually, the men are put on trial, and Houston must defend them in the only way he can—not guilty by reason of senility. He doesn't want to do this to the men; as he tells Judge Gurney before the trial starts, these are three of the men who took Texas away from Santa Ana.

In court, the fictional Houston employed oratory that surely recalled at least the spirit of the real-life lawyer himself.

Houston urges the jury not to persecute the old men. Houston calls them ancient warriors and tells the court, and by extension society itself, that their day has come and gone, and they should be pitied, and society should shed a tear for what the men once were.

The speech is eloquent, even elegant, in its prose.

The old men are acquitted, but are left angry and bitter at Houston. It falls to Taggart to tell them the truth. He reminds them that without Houston's defense of them, they would have ended up in the gallows, guilty of treason. Taggart reminds the men that by tearing them down in public, Houston was also tearing down his own father, the revered Sam Houston, to save their lives.[20]

It has been argued that even if the Hollywood depiction of the West wasn't completely accurate, film and television westerns at least gave viewers a feel for the times and the people who inhabited those years. "Sam's Boy" was one of the episodes where *Temple Houston* did that most admirably.

§

ENDNOTES

1. *Western Clippings,* page 8.
2. Williams, pages 9, 15, and 16.
3. Rose, page 26.
4. "The Twisted Rope," script courtesy of Jack Turley.
5. Jarvis, page 212
6. Jarvis, page 213
7. "The Twisted Rope," script courtesy of Jack Turley
8. "Jubilee," broadcast November 14, 1963, written by John Robinson and Paul Savage; "Letter of the Law," broadcast October 3, 1963, written by Donald S. Sanford.
9. "Gallows at Galilee," written by E.M.Parsons, Warner Bros. Archive, University of Southern California, Los Angeles.
10. "Toll the Bell Slowly," written by Robert Leslie Bellem and Carey Wilbur, Warner Bros. Archive, University of Southern California, Los Angeles.
11. "The Dark Madonna," written by Gerry Day, Warner Bros. Archive, University of Southern California, Los Angeles.
12. "The Town That Trespassed," script courtesy of Jack Turley.
13. The second half of this episode was acquired on video, collector to collector, for home viewing.
14. Gardner, page 55
15. "Enough Rope," written by Robert Vincent Wright, and "Fracas at Kiowa Flats," written by Carey Wilbur, Warner Bros. Archive, University of Southern California, Los Angeles.
16. Ibid
17. Merlman, page 66.
18. "Ten Rounds for Baby," written by William R. Cox, Warner Bros. Archive, University of Southern California, Los Angeles.
19. "Toll the Bell Slowly," written by Robert Leslie Bellum and Carey Wilbur, Warner Bros. Archive, University of Southern California, Los Angeles.
20. "Sam's Boy," written by Warren Douglas, Warner Bros. Archive, University of Southern California, Los Angeles.

Chapter Seven
The Robert Taylor Show

When the producers of *The Robert Taylor Show* received word on July 17th that the show was being cancelled by NBC even before it premiered, they wanted to get word to their star before he heard about it some other way—a common occurrence in Hollywood, where many television actors tell stories about reading the announcement of the cancellation of their series in the newspaper before being told in person.

In this case, the producers were determined to get to Taylor first.

Taylor, however, was a bit hard to track down—he was in Wyoming, fishing, something he loved to do.

"Oh, my God," Taylor said, upon hearing the news. "That poor crew. What will they do?"[1]

Taylor's first reaction was sympathy for the crewmembers, committed to a newly defunct series, and who might now find it virtually impossible to find work for months, as all the other shows were staffed.

"That was Taylor," series writer Christopher Knopf said. "A thoroughly decent, compassionate fellow. We all loved and admired him hugely."[2]

There had been a lot of excitement about the series among those working on it; there was a feeling they had something special. That's also why there was so much disappointment was the rug was pulled out from under them.

The Robert Taylor Show was a reworking of a 1962 episode of Four Star's *The Dick Powell Show* called "330 Independence SW," starring William Bendix, Julie Adams, and David McLean. The episode, with Bendix as a truck driver who runs afoul of the US Department of Health, Education, and Welfare by selling illegal pills to teenagers and other drivers, was written by Allan Sloane and directed by Sam Fuller. It aired March 20, 1962, as the 25th episode of the first season of the Powell anthology program, a highly honored and respected series known not only for its high-quality presentations, but also for the potential pilots among its episodes.

Taylor had been intrigued by the idea and agreed to star in the series as Christopher Logan, a special assistant to the Secretary of HEW; The Secretary would remain unnamed, in hopes the series would continue no matter what administration was serving in the real White House. HEW in 1963 employed 60,000 people to, Taylor told reporters, help "the American people help themselves toward a healthier and more secure world." [3]

When he committed to the series, Taylor had two stipulations. He wanted most of his summers free (so that he could pursue the outdoor activities he loved, like hunting and fishing) and he especially didn't want to shoot in Washington, D.C., in August, saying the muggy weather sapped his energy. But the star quickly gave in on both requests.

"I didn't even put up a fight," Taylor said. "Why? Well, the more scripts I read, the more excited I get about this series.

"Christopher Knopf is doing one on Indian health; Tom Gries, employment of the aged; Gwen Bagni, unadoptable children; John Dunkel, typhoid; Cliff Gould, the rehabilitation of the mentally ill. I could go on and on."[4]

Taylor believed the series could be both provocative and entertaining. He would also narrate, and episodes would take a semi-documentary approach; scenes would be shot in any city where the HEW conducted its investigations, including Washington, D.C.

As had been his trademark throughout his Hollywood career, Taylor took a no-nonsense approach to work on the series, and always appreciated the work of the writers and crew around him. "Actors like to make their profession sound overly complicated," he told reporters. "All I do is memorize the lines and get them on film as quickly and convincingly as I can.

"More important for an actor than high-sounding theorizing is that he surround himself with creative and skilled specialists in production. I've done that and, if we have a good show, they merit the lion's share of credit."[5]

The production team for the show was indeed top notch. Bruce Geller and Bernard Kowalski were running the show, and production personnel included producer Merwin Gerard, directors John Newland and John Cassavetes, and assistant producer Dennis Shyryack. All were film and television veterans with years of experience under their belts.

The pilot was written by Bruce Geller and directed by Bernard Kowalski. Taylor starred in a story about a plague victim in Los Angeles, and the desperate search to find him before the plague could spread. Taylor's Logan was the older, more conservative, agency veteran, and actor Robert Loggia, as his right hand man, played a younger, and more liberal character, a combination designed to give the episodes added dramatic punch.[6]

Loggia backed out after completing the pilot through a technicality in his contract when the series, which had working titles of *330 Independence SW* and *The Quiet War*, was renamed *The Robert Taylor Show*. Actor George Segal was signed to replace him.[7]

The original pick-up for the series was for thirteen episodes, standard network practice in 1963.

The series went into production, and the first scripts and episodes came down off the Four Star assembly line. That's when the trouble started.

When *The Robert Taylor Show* was announced for NBC's fall 1963 schedule, it was said to have the cooperation of the HEW and its stories would be based on official case files. "We flew to Washington and had the cooperation of the HEW," director Bernard Kowalski said.[8]

However, a press spokesman for HEW said in July that the agency had never officially endorsed the series and that inaccuracies had been found in two of the episodes already produced.

"We have given no permission for official department endorsement," the spokesman told *The New York Times*. "We have been cooperating with Four Star and had a written understanding with them to the effect that we would provide information and review services.

"But the series is their responsibility and we stipulated that they could make no attribution of stories as coming from official department files."

HEW also said that the show failed to give enough recognition to the role that state organizations had in helping HEW operations. HEW seemed especially concerned about this point; the spokesman said the department had "a few" solely federal operations but that most of its work was conducted through a federal-state partnership.

"It became apparent," the spokesman said, "after viewing scripts, that some of these basic inaccuracies were of a continuing nature.

"You do not inject a federal agency or representative into a situation in a wrong way. In many of these situations, investigation is the work of the state official."[9]

The spokesman said he didn't know anything about reports that members of Congress had been criticizing HEW, saying the department was working on the series to gain publicity.

Four Star President Tom McDermott had met with HEW officials on July 17th, to talk about ways to improve the working relationship.

Eventually, McDermott issued a terse statement, saying, "We are not in breach of our agreement with the production of *The Robert Taylor Show* and we are now, as we have been in the past, prepared to meet our obligations in all respects.

"We have always had the cooperation of the department and recently we went to Washington to improve our liaison…and discussing the procedures of a closer working relationship with the department."

The spokesman for HEW said McDermott had been cooperative at that meeting; McDermott had said Four Star would take HEW's suggestions for changes in the episodes under advisement.[10]

NBC said that it had cancelled the series because the show had no official government blessing.

Those working on the series always felt there were other motives at work. "Several scripts were ordered and they really got into sensitive areas," Christopher Knopf said. "Bruce was taking very liberal positions about what was wrong in this country in social areas of deprivation and ignorance, and before the show ever got on the air, NBC panicked and said, 'Well, we just can't put this thing on.'"[11]

For example, in the episode scripted by Knopf, "A New Day is Dying," William Shatner guest-starred as a Native American doctor working in a reservation clinic, married to a Caucasian nurse, and concealing the fact that he is of Native American origin. One of the conflicts the character is facing was between himself, as a man of modern medicine, and the Indian medicine man, to whom most of the Indians turned. His wife makes a mistake with a medical prescription, with devastating consequences for their patient, and their marriage.[12]

"It was about the time that HEW was coming out with their bans on cigarettes and various other products," Bernard Kowalski, who directed "A New Day is Dying," said. "To the best of my knowledge, big business stepped in and said, 'we don't want to create an image for HEW so that when it speaks, someone of the stature and integrity of Robert Taylor is gonna give it all the more meaning.'"[13]

"We were never given a real reason for being pulled," Taylor said, about a year later. "But I think NBC did it because of certain actions taken by the Department of Health, Education, and Welfare in the area of food and drugs, like the reports on cigarette smoking. They must have thought twice about having a series on the network which was based on the government agency attacking their big sponsors.

"I thought it was an unforgivable action by NBC…they didn't look at any of (the episodes) and they never gave us a reason for their doing what they did."[14]

It was reported that four episodes of *The Robert Taylor Show* had been produced, in addition to the pilot, and that NBC and Four Star had spent about $100,000 on each and hundreds of thousands of dollars more on series development and production.

THE ROBERT TAYLOR SHOW

"We did four shows," George Segal, who played Nick, said. "All good scripts."[15]

The episodes, in various stages of development and/or production at the time of cancellation, included "A New Day is Dying," as described above; "Success Story," written by Bruce Geller, directed by Bernard Kowalski, and guest-starring Michael Parks, Joanna Moore, and John Larkin; "Hiram," written by Tom Seller, directed by Barney Girard, and guest starring Ernest Truex, Jack Mullaney, and Estelle Winwood; and "Shadows of the World Appear," written by Lawrence Edward Watkin, directed by Kowalski, and guest starring Lawrence Dobkin, Luanna Anders, and Peter Helm. Additional scripts included those written by Leonard Freeman (his was titled "Once Upon a Time"), Gwen Bagni, John Dunkel, Tom Gries, and Cliff Gould.[16]

It should also be noted that there were those in the television industry who believed that NBC had economic concerns about the show. This was an issue in the industry that year; ABC had come close to pulling its new series *Channing*, about life on a college campus, before it ever aired, for lack of advertiser interest. The difference between the two was that *Channing* already had thirteen episodes completed and the investment was too much for ABC to back out of.

At the time the Taylor series was pulled off the fall schedule, its advertising inventory was about half sold. Advertisers were apparently thinking twice about story lines involving federal investigations of drugs, foods, and health issues.

The series had lined up Buick, Heinz, Pharmacraft, S.C. Johnson, Lehr & Fink, MGM, Helena Rubinstein, and Sherwin Williams in what were described as "comparatively small buys."

But as soon as *Temple Houston* was announced as the replacement for *The Robert Taylor Show*, Bristol-Meyers and Goodyear made buys, and five of the sponsors from the Taylor series—Buick, Heinz, Pharmacraft, S.C. Johnson, and Lehr & Fink—moved into *Temple Houston*, as well.

Temple Houston was a better seller in a few weeks than *The Robert Taylor Show* had been in several months. That, for NBC, represented the bottom line and a way out from under the HEW controversy and its concerns about the show.[17]

"The controversial subjects might have scared off some sponsors," George Segal recalled later.[18]

Still, NBC's cancellation of the Four Star Taylor production caught everyone, including Robert Taylor, by surprise. "Everything in the world that could go wrong has gone wrong," he told a friend.[19] *The New York Times* reported that the "cancellation so close to the starting date was considered unusual."[20]

"It was a shock," Segal said.[21]

There was some talk at Four Star about finding a different home for the series, but it had become a bit of a hot potato and might have represented a legal hassle in terms of being picked up by another network. The episodes were never broadcast.

"It didn't sour me on television, per se," Taylor said, "But it sure made me gun shy on the validity of contracts. You're apparently just as safe in gambling on a pilot as in having a firm, non-cancelable contract with a network."[22]

Not even a star of Robert Taylor's magnitude was immune to the ups and downs of network television. He would feel the sting again just a few months later, when Four Star was preparing a television pilot called *The Four Lions*, a proposed one-hour dramatic series for the 1964–65 season about family members with four different occupations. Taylor, Robert Wagner, and Brandon de Wilde had been cast when network indifference stopped the project in its tracks before production started on the pilot. [23]

Taylor would have to wait until 1966 to again find lasting success on television, when he became host and occasional star of the syndicated western series *Death Valley Days*. It was a job the actor loved and one he held until his death, from lung cancer, in 1969.

The cancellation of *The Robert Taylor Show* came at a time when Four Star, which had been among the most successful and most important independent production studios, was going through a difficult period. In many ways, the best days of Four Star were behind it.

Its president, Dick Powell, had died on January 2, 1963, at the age of 58. Powell, the long-time Hollywood actor, producer, and media mogul, had fashioned Four Star into an immensely profitable and prosperous company, sometimes using only the force of his own personality to make deals and hold things together. At its height, Four Star filled hours and hours of primetime television programming every week, season after season, on the three networks.

Christopher Knopf recalled later that, "things were growing sticky at Four Star. With no Dick Powell to run interference, shows began to wane and crumble."[24]

McDermott, a former advertising agency executive, had been brought into the business by Powell in 1959 and began to handle much of the company's day-to-day business. McDermott was company president while Powell was chairman of the board. He took over the full reigns of the company after Powell's death, but he did not engender the same feelings of loyalty among writers, producers, and actors that Powell had, many of whom believed that Dick Powell was Four Star.

Knopf, who recounted a major blow-up with McDermott, wrote later that, "As for Four Star, at the time of Dick Powell's death it had a dozen shows on the air, give or take one. Two years later it had two. A year after that, just one, *The Big Valley*, which played on ABC for four years."[25]

One of the "What ifs" in this story is the question of whether or not Dick Powell could have saved *The Robert Taylor Show*. Could he have stepped in, as he had in other instances in the past with sponsors, network executives, etc., and smoothed over concerns? Could he have cajoled more sponsors into signing onboard, and convinced those sponsors already signed to continue to back the series? He'd done it before.

If so, the inclusion of the Taylor series on NBC's fall schedule would have given Warner Bros. and Jeff Hunter's Apollo Productions more time to properly prepare *Temple Houston*.

In the end the decisions made by NBC in July 1963 had wide-ranging impact. Consider: instead of having one unaired series (Taylor's show) and one unsuccessful series (Hunter's show) on its hands, NBC might have had two successful franchises on its schedule. It's possible the television arms at both Four Star and Warner Bros. would have been strengthened in the process.

The careers of Jack Webb and Jeff Hunter were also negatively impacted by the decision—Webb was fired from Warner Bros. that December, and Hunter's hopes for a successful series and career boost were dashed.

As for the bewildered cast and crew of *The Robert Taylor Show*, they had no choice but to go on to other projects, inside and outside of Four Star, as best they could. "We were all paid off," Kowalski said. [26]

§

ENDNOTES

1. Knopf, e-mail.
2. Ibid
3. Purcelli, page C 4
4. Grant, "Bob Taylor Back on TV With Exciting News Series," page 6 G
5. Purcelli, page C 4
6. Knopf, e-mail.
7. Kleiner, "Loggia Knows How to Fail by Really Trying," page 31
8. White, page 4
9. Sheperd, page 55
10. Ibid
11. White, page 4
12. Knopf, e-mail
13. White, page 4
14. Stern, "Robert Taylor One Actor Not Afraid to Speak up," page 5 G
15. Hopper, "Bruno, the Sexy Banjo Player," page 29
16. Bruce Geller Papers, Performing Arts Special Collections, University of California Los Angeles, Los Angeles

17. *Television Age,* August 5, 1963, page 17.

18. Heimer, page 3

19. Wayne, page 214

20. Sheperd, page 55

21. Hopper, "Bruno, the Sexy Banjo Player," page 29

22. Stern, "Robert Taylor One Actor Not Afraid to Speak up," page 5 G

23. *Television Age,* November 25, 1963

24. Knopf, page 72

25. Knopf, pages 74, 76

26. White, page 4

Chapter Eight
Postscript

When *Temple Houston* premiered on September 19, 1963, the program description in *TV Guide* began with, "Two of television's sure fire ingredients—the Law and the West—are combined in this 60 minute dramatic series about a circuit-riding attorney in the early southwest."[1]

As it turned out, there was nothing "sure fire" about the series, except for the popularity of its two stars. And, truth be told, the lawyer and the Western hadn't always been a good mix.

In Western films, it was the sheriff, or the marshal, often standing alone against the violence and lawlessness of criminals, most often represented the law. As pointed out in *The BFI Companion to the Western*, "It's not the lawyer but the sheriff who represents the law, who is the 'lawman,' and who stands not only for the law but, in a synecdochal relationship, for civilization itself."[2]

In Westerns on television, the lawyer as hero made out a little better. The lawyer-hero was represented not only in *Temple Houston*, but also in other series, such as *Black Saddle*, as well as in dozens of episodes of other westerns on television where a guest star played an able attorney. Arguably, the most successful lawyer-hero on a television Western was Jarrod Barkley, as portrayed by Richard Long on *The Big Valley* from 1965–69. The law was an integral part of many episodes of the series and Barkley was often featured in and out of the courtroom defending clients and arguing the right and wrong about public policies and finer points of the law.[3]

Temple Houston's place in the pantheon of Western dramas lies in the attempt to combine the best elements of both the legal drama and the Western. The series, as indicated in one of the earliest memos at Warner Brothers about the show, fell somewhere between *Perry Mason*, *Cheyenne*, and *Maverick*. *The New York Times* caught it about right in 1964 when it ran a photo from the series with a caption that said, "Jeff Hunter plays a circuit-riding lawyer on the Old Frontier, who fights injustice everywhere and only occasionally pleads cases before a jury."[4]

Temple Houston's place is the career of Jeffrey Hunter is secure; it is the only series he headlined during his lifetime, and he went into the project excited about the character and the series itself. "I think it's a good role for me," the actor said early in the show's run.[5]

American popular culture can often be cruel; for a leading man like Hunter, a one season television series is often viewed as a dismal failure, while for a character actor like co-star Jack Elam, it is simply viewed as another job in a long line of jobs. Elam was allowed to move on to other parts without the weight of a failed series weighing on his career, while Hunter was left to ponder issues of career momentum.

As to the format changes in the series, and whether the changes helped or hurt the series, it depends, as always, on one's perspective. There are those, including Hunter, who believed the changes helped the series, but there are also those who wrote at the time that the changes didn't help the series at all. Neither format emphasis was a ratings success.

Jeffrey Hunter and Jack Elam, 1963.
(Photofest)

Interviewed in the summer of 1965, as he was guest starring in the series premiere of *The FBI*, Hunter perhaps betrayed his roots as a film actor when he said of *Temple Houston*, "The trouble was that too many people got into the act—everybody had a different idea. Television series should be the work of one man—a dictator—who knows what he wants and gets it."[6]

In the end, the legacy of the men and women who produced, wrote, and acted in *Temple Houston* is that somehow, some way, the series premiered as scheduled, on time, at 7:30 pm, September 19, 1963, and that twenty-five other episodes rolled off the Warner Bros. assembly line, as well. With the astonishing obstacles thrown at them, this was no small achievement.

Temple Houston was described in one review as a "grade C Western,"[7] a description that simply fails to consider the fact that the series was rushed into production. But either way, the grade for the people who did the best they could to produce the series, under the circumstances, was A plus.

One of the most intriguing what-ifs about *Temple Houston* was whether it actually had found its voice toward the end of the season, as Hunter believed, and whether future seasons would have meant better things for the production, with more time to prepare episodes.

"I enjoyed working on the series," Jeffrey Hunter said, "and learned a lot about TV."[8]

§

ENDNOTES

1. *TV Guide,* September 19, 1963, page A- 62.

2. Buscombe, page 171

3. See the episode broadcast on October 30, 1965, "The Odyssey of Jubal Tanner," written by Paul Savage, as just one example.

4. *The New York Times,* picture cutline, February 16, 1964, page X- 17.

5. MacMinn, page D 2

6. Kleiner, "Hunter: TV Needs Dictators," page 7

7. Lowry, "Some Fall Shows Already on the Ropes," page 3

8. Pruess, page 29

Appendix A
Temple Houston Episode Guide

Temple Houston was produced by The Temple Houston Company, a joint venture between Apollo Productions, Inc., Roncom Productions, Inc., and Warner Bros. Pictures for the NBC Television Network. The series ran from September 19, 1963 through September 16, 1964, including repeats. 26 episodes were shot in black & white on film. The series was scheduled by NBC to air on Thursday nights at 7:30 pm throughout its network run.

Executive producers: Jack Webb, William T. Orr, Jeffrey Hunter (uncredited, through Apollo Productions); producers: Joseph Dackow, Richard M. Bluel; Story Consultant: Thomas Thompson; associate producers: Lawrence Dobkin, Jimmy Lydon; Music: Frank Perkins, Frank Comstock, Ned Washington; Director of Photography: Robert Hoffman; Cinematography: Ralph Woolsey; Operator: Al Green; Assistant Cameraman: Al Baalas; Script Supervisor: Howard Hubler; Gaffer: Leroy Thompson; Best Boy: Michael Monk; Grip: Weldon Gilbert; Prop Man: Robert Lamb; Mixer: B.F. Ryan; Wardrobe (M): Pat Kelly; Wardrobe: Helen Racken; Art Direction: Carl Macauley, Perry Ferguson; Set Director: Ralph S. Hurst; Film Editor: Stefan Arnsten, Byron Chudnow; Sound: Samuel F. Goode; Makeup Supervisor: George Bau; Supervising Hair Stylist: Jean Burt Reilly; Hair Stylist: Carla Hadley; Set Decorator: William L. Kuehl; Assistant Director: William Kissel, C. Carter Gibson; Second Assistant Director: Al Alleborn; Series produced under the personal supervision of Jack Warner.

Participating sponsors: Goodyear, Beechnut, Heinz, R.J. Reynolds, Vicks, Goodrich, Proctor & Gamble, Breck, Lehn & Fink, Helena Rubenstein, others.

Cast: Jeffrey Hunter (Temple Houston, Attorney at Law); Jack Elam (U.S. Deputy Marshal George Taggart). Recurring cast: James Best (Gotch); Mary Wickes (Ida Goff), Frank Ferguson (Judge Gurney), Chubby Johnson (Concho).

Synopsis: The exploits of Temple Houston, the son of Sam Houston, in the Southwest during the 1880s, with many episodes set specifically in towns such as Tascosa and Lindley, Texas. Houston, a circuit court lawyer, takes on both civil and criminal cases.

The following episode guide includes information about all 26 episodes, including titles, writers, directors, crew, and guest stars. Episode descriptions and other information were culled from scripts, production information, and publicity found in the Warner Bros. Archive; newspaper summaries, and *TV Guide* program listings.

Author's notes on individual episodes are also included, and may refer to the episode itself or the series in general.

1.A. Temple Houston TV Pilot.

Unaired in its original form. Written by Michael S. Zagor and Dean Reisner. Directed by William Conrad. Executive Producer: Jack Webb. Produced by Michael Meshekoff. Filming began on March 12, 1963, and ended on March 21, 1963.

Stars: Jeffrey Hunter (Temple Houston); Preston Foster (Judge Homer Black); and James Coburn (Boyd Palmer).

Guest Stars: Joanna Moore (Rita Dillard); Edward Andrews (Hyde); Ed Nelson (Cole Marteen); Grace Lee Whitney (Texas Rose); Kevin Hagen (John Dillard); Karl Swenson (Sheriff).

Synopsis: In Tascosa, Texas, Temple Houston defends the husband of a former girlfriend who has been accused of murder. In the pilot the audience sees the first evidence that the character of Houston will be highly fictionalized, as Houston does whatever he has to do, shady or not, to defend his client. This story included having Marshal Boyd Palmer falsely arrested and hiring a pickpocket to steal a witness' watch, both done to gain enough time to prove his client's innocence.

Notes: The pilot for the series was never seen on television in its original form, though it was successful in selling the series to NBC. Later released to movie theatres as part of various double bills, the film, retitled *The Man From Galveston*, failed to generate much box office interest. To avoid confusion with the weekly series, dialogue was looped in referring to the main character as 'Timothy Higgins.' See separate entry following the episode guide.

1.B. Temple Houston TV Pilot # 2.

Unaired. Written by James Warner Bellah. Directed by William Conrad. Produced by Jack Webb. One day of shooting was done on June 13, 1963.

Stars: Jeffrey Hunter (Temple Houston); Jack Elam (George Taggart).

Notes: This was a series of color and black and white photographic and sound tests. 290 feet of color film was shot; 3,420 feet of black and white film was shot.

1.C. Temple Houston Promotional Spot.

Written by Alan Hirschfeld. Directed by Jack Webb. Produced by Joseph Dackow. One day of shooting was done on August 14, 1963.

Stars: Jeffrey Hunter, Jack Elam, and Jack Webb.

Synopsis: The promotional spot featured Jack Webb touting the high production values of the series, including the motion picture style production, the scripts from veteran writers, and the veteran directors. Webb said the series would be fresh and have a new look because it would be using six Western streets, twenty seven interior sets, and that scenes would be shot on location as needed. The promo included scenes from the original series pilot and from the first episode of the series, "The Twisted Rope." Hunter and Elam also appeared as themselves, although in costume and ostensibly 'between scenes,' speaking with Webb about the high quality of the series.

Notes: The pitch was shot on the Western Street location at Warner Brothers, and on an interior soundstage. The script for the promo was nine pages long.[1]

1.D. Temple Houston Main Titles.

Directed by Lawrence Dobkin. Produced by Joseph Dackow. One day of shooting was done on August 16, 1963.

Stars: Jeffrey Hunter, Jack Elam.

Synopsis: The series titles included a sequence in which Temple Houston shoots Marshal Taggart's boot spur, causing it to spin, followed by the two men smiling and riding off down the street together.

Notes: Location work for the main titles included open country at the Iverson Ranch and the Western Street at Warner Bros.. The shoot required the use of seventeen extras, including ten horses and two dogs.

1.1 The Twisted Rope. September 19, 1963.

Written by Jack Turley, from a story by James Warner Bellah. Directed by Abner Biberman. Executive Producer: Jack Webb. Produced by Joseph Dackow. Filming began on August 7, 1963, and ended on August 16, 1963.

Guest Stars: Victory Jory (Claude Boley), Collin Wilcox (Dorrie Chevenix), Booth Colman, Richard Evans (Roan Chevenix), Anthony D. Call (Conch Chevenix).

Bits: Bill Zuckert, Hal Smith, Sarah Selby, Robert Shaw, James Drum, Paul Newlan, Dan Dillaway, Thor Biberman, Charles Fredericks, Jim Boles.

Stunts: John Harris, Byron Fromme.

Synopsis: The Chevenix brothers have been accused of murdering the sheriff, and their sister asks Temple Houston to defend them. Houston faces a race against time, as angry townspeople want to hang the accused.

Notes: The working title for this episode was "Two Murders at Noon." Hunter was paid for eight days, a total of $7,000.

1.2 Find Angel Chavez. September 26, 1963.

Written by John Hawkins and Steve McNeil. Directed by Herman Hoffman. Executive Producer: Jack Webb. Produced by Joseph Dackow. Filming began on August 19, 1963, and ended on August 27, 1963.

Guest Stars: Rafael Campos (Angel Chavez), Edmund Vargas, Linda Dangcil (Maria), Woodrow Parfrey (Fred Bell), Gene Evans (Sam Clanton), Ben Wright, Anna Navarro (Donna Lennox), Herbert Rudley (Paul Lennox), Lane Bradford, Rico Alanzz, John Truax.

Bits: Forrest Lewis, Alex Montoya, Roberto Contreras.

Synopsis: Marshal Taggart has been framed for murder; he says it was self-defense. His defense counsel: Temple Houston. Houston must find the sheepherder who was a witness to the killing.

Notes: The working title for this episode was "The Guns of Troy." Hunter was paid $5,000 for seven days work.

1.3 Letter of the Law. October 3, 1963.

Written by Donald S. Sanford. Directed by Robert Totten. Executive Producer: Jack Webb. Produced by Joseph Dackow. Filming began on September 9, 1963, and ended September 17, 1963.

Guest stars: James Anderson (Vint Harrod), Victor French (Willie Harrod), Jan Stine (Prue Harrod), Del Monroe, Edward Platt, Hayden Rorke (Pinkley),

Brenda Scott (Ruth), Trevot Bardette, William Fawcett, Chahan Denton (Judge Denton), Richard Cutting, H.M. Wynant (Jered Mallory), and Terry Frost.

Bits: Loyss Bradley, James Stone, Art Stewart, Olivia M. Baker (sideline musician), Eugene Le Pique (practical musician).

Stunts: Jerry Brown, Byron Fromme, Bob Herron, Clyde Hudkins, Buzz Henry.

Synopsis: Houston faces a moral dilemma as he defends the Harrod brothers on criminal charges: he believes one of the three men to be guilty. Two of the brothers, one a no-good and the other an innocent, are shielding the real murderer. Houston has to separate the innocent out from the guilty.

Notes: NBC's trade magazine ads for the series featured an artist's sketch of one of the publicity photos of Jeff Hunter and described the character as "Laconic. Temple Houston is the least talkative lawyer in television. Though he can deliver a fine oration, NBC's young saddle-and-spurs solicitor is generally short on words, long on action."[2]

1.4 Toll the Bell Slowly.

Written by Robert Leslie Bellum and Carey Wilbur. Directed by Gerd Oswald. Executive Producer: Jack Webb. Produced by: Joseph Dackow. Filming began August 28, 1963, and ended September 6, 1963.

Guest stars: Everett Sloane (Daniel Forbes), Leo Gordon (Charles Grimm), Walter Burke (Potts), Carlos Rivero, Royal Dano (Sheriff Smiley), Robert Adler, Noah Beery (Bailey), Rusty Lane (Poag), Susan Kohner (Ellena Romolo), Joseph Brooks, Charles Morton, Jack O'Shea, Felipe Turich, and James Bell (Dr. David Carter).

Bits: Orville Sherman, Robert Faulk, George Barrows, Mark Conrad, C. Alvin Bell.

Stunts: Emmet North, Byron Fromme, Rick Warrick.

Synopsis: Houston and Taggart ride into a town searching for a man who can help clear Houston's client of a murder charge. Houston finds his alibi witness, all right—in jail, sentenced to hang for murder, and Houston has just hours to save the man's life so that he can testify in the other trial. Houston discovers that the killing stemmed from a fight over a local waitress.

Notes: The working title for the episode was "Trail Hands are for Hanging." Hunter was paid for eight days on this episode, $5,500.

1.5 The Third Bullet. October 24, 1963.

Written by Antony Ellis. Directed by Alvin Ganzer. Executive Producer: Jack Webb. Produced by Joseph Dackow. Filming began on September 25, 1963, and ended September 26, 1963.

Guest stars: Anne Helm (Francie), Frank Sutton (Logan Stocker), Hampton Fancher (Jim Stocker), Don Beddoe (Simpson), George Petrie (Newton Fountain), and Parley Baer (Sheriff Beckman).

Bits: Ralph Moody, Joe Maguinn, Al Paige, Jim Hayward, Clyde Hudkins, Norman Leavitt, Bob Herron, King Mojave, George DeNormano, George Bell, Frank Sully, Joe Brown, and Jack Shea.

Synopsis: In the wide-open town of Salton, Temple Houston defends Jim Stocker, who's been arrested by Deputy U.S. Marshal George Taggart for robbery and murder. Taggart pursues a romance with Stocker's fiancée as Houston tries to win a new hearing for his client. Francie Terrell and Jim's brother Logan help Jim break jail when the case goes against him.

Notes: Hunter essentially had two costume changes as Temple Houston; he wore buckskins on the trail and a frocked coat and striped trousers in court.[3]

1.6 Gallows in Galilee. October 31, 1963.

Written by E. M. Parsons. Directed by Robert Totten. Executive Producer: Jack Webb. Produced by Joseph Dackow. Filming began September 27, 1963, and ended October 4, 1963. Hunter recalled for pickup shots on October 11, 1963.

Guest stars: Robert Lansing (Judge Galen Stark), Jacqueline Scott (Kate Hagadorn), Tol Avery (Eli Bascombe), Elisha Cook, Jr. (John Alvorsen), Dabbs Greer (Marshal Cloud), Ralph Reed (Roy Julian), Bob Steele (Yeager), and Richard Grant (Ainslee Priest).

Bits: Andy Albin, Joe Polina, Dan Cass, Ted French, Pedro Regas, Hal Barringer, Mike Mondhan, Ted Moriclans, Jerry Brown.

Synopsis: Houston defends an innocent young man charged with murder, but the case is being heard before a judge known for his harsh sentences. The judge tosses key evidence that Houston believes clears his client. As the case proceeds, the town is engulfed with prejudice against the young man. Houston and Taggart dig into the background of the judge to see if they can discover what turned him into a 'hanging judge.'

Notes: The working title for the episode was "Build My Gallows High." Hunter was paid $5,000 for seven days work.

1.7 The Siege at Thayer's Bluff. November 7, 1963.

Written by Preston Wood. Directed by Alvin Ganzer. Executive Producer: Jack Webb. Produced by Joseph Dackow. Filming began October 7, 1963, and ended October 14, 1963.

Guest stars: Russ Thorsen (Red Gilman), Bob Bray (Hal Kester), John Cliff (Joe Joyce), Nina Shipman (Mary Bannerman), William Reynolds (Paul Bannerman), E. J. Andre (Judge Diversey), Shug Fisher (Augie Wren).

Bits: Bob Herron, Byron Fromme, Louise Elias, Bill Hart, John Harris, Tom Sweet, and Billy Shannon.

Synopsis: Rancher Red Gitman and his hired guns are after miner Paul Bannerman and his wife, who have squatter's rights on land Gitman claims belongs to him. Houston risks his life to defend the couple, but Bannerman not only turns his guns on Gitman, but Houston, as well.

Notes: Director Alvin Ganzer said Jeff Hunter was "good in westerns."[4] Hunter was paid $5,000 for seven days work.

1.8 Jubilee. November 14, 1963.

Written by Paul Savage and John Robinson. Directed by Robert Totten. Executive Producer: Jack Webb. Produced by: Joseph Dackow. Filming began October 15, 1963, and ended October 23, 1963.

Guest stars: Joe Howarth, Mills Watson, William Bromley (Ford Conley), Peter Whitney (Cletus Emory), Paul Birch (Matt Clendennon), Virginia Gregg (Elizabeth Clendennon), Dub Taylor (Cliff Willard), Eddie Firestone (Tobe Gillard), Morgan Woodward (Sheriff Ivers), and Ian Wolf (Judge Farnley).

Bits: Hal Torey, Clyde Howdy, Buzz Henry.

Stunts: Alex Sharpe, Byron Fromme, Bob Herron, Buzz Henry, Jerry Brown, Clyde Hudkins.

Synopsis: Houston and Taggart save Tobe Gillard from a lynch mob, but then discover that Gillard has been accused of killing one of Houston's friends. To get at the truth, Houston makes the difficult and unpopular decision to defend the accused.

Notes: The working title for the episode was "No Justice at Jubilee." Hunter was paid $5,000 for seven days work.

1.9 Thunder Gap. November 21, 1963.

Written by Harold Jack Bloom, Preston Wood, and Thomas Thompson. Directed by Leslie H. Martinson. Executive Producer: Jack Webb. Produced by Joseph Dackow. Filming began October 29, 1963, and ended November 5, 1963.

Guest stars: Diana Millay (Marcey Bannister), Barbara Knudson, Pat Rosson, John Pickard, Robert Colbert (Tom Bannister), Brad Weston (Lew Sykes), Tom Skerritt, Alex Sharpe, Richard Garland (Jess Newmark), Harry Lauter (Sheriff Macon), Gregg Palmer.

Bits: Mae Boss, Alan Reynolds.

Stunts: Byron Fromme, Joe Yrigoyen.

Synopsis: Marcey Bannister, traveling west to see her husband, doesn't believe that he's an outlaw—not even when he and a friend try to rob a stagecoach she's riding on. Houston and Taggart must protect her, her desperado husband, and another outlaw from a posse out for vengeance.

Notes: The working title for the episode was "Five Fugitives." Hunter's pay was seven days, $5,000.

1.10 Billy Hart. November 28, 1963.

Written by Herman Groves and Norman Jolley. Directed by William Conrad. Executive Producer: Jack Webb. Produced by Joseph Dackow. Filming began on November 6, 1963 and ended on November 12, 1963.

Guest stars: Audrey Dalton (Amy Hart), Ron Hayes (Lambert), John Lormer (Matt Turner), Pat Cardi (Billy Hart), Russ Conway (Henry Hart), J.H. Philip Ober (Bert Clarke).

Bits: Rhys Williams (Judge Curry), Len Lesser (Orley Baldwin), Jack Cardl, Art Koulias (Desk Clerk), George Neise (Amos Tromp), Dorothy Konrad (Emma Bryant), James Nusser (Flytrap).

Synopsis: Amy Hart's husband has died and he has left her with another problem. In his will, he left his property, as well as custody of their child, to his ranch foreman. Houston is forced to carry out the provisions of the will.

Notes: The working title for the episode was "The Amy Hart Story." Hunter was paid for seven days, $5,000.

1.11 Seventy Times Seven. December 5, 1963.

Written by Arthur Browne, Jr., and D.D. Beauchamp. Directed by Robert Totten. Executive Producer: Jack Webb. Produced by Richard M. Bluel. Filming began on November 13, 1963, and ended on November 15, 1963.

Guest stars: Susan Cramer (Helmi Bergen), Fay Wall, Sam Edwards (Bartender), Simon Scott (Sheriff Hab Martin), Steve Ihnat (Ben Wade), Karl Swenson (Sam Wade), Tom Holland (Lee Bates), Don Stafford (Fritz Bergen), Thomas Hubbard, Hans Gudegast, James Alamanzar, Robert Rothwell (Joe Shivers), Lane Chandler, Werner Reichow, Walter Mathews (Prosecutor), Charles Radilac (Gustav Bergen), Marshall Bradford (Judge).

Bits: Ray Hoback (piano), Breena Howard, Rick Warick, Buzz Henry, Emile Avery, Clyde Hudkins, Mae Boss, Jerry Brown.

Stunts: Buzz Henry.

Synopsis: Ben Wade keeps bullying peace-loving Gustav Bergen and his family, who refuse to fight back because their religion forbids violence. Houston intervenes in the farmer-cattlemen war by getting a court order naming Taggart as the family's official defender.

Notes: Hunter said that no matter what costume he wore, Temple Houston always wore boots. "In deference to courtroom etiquette, though, I always remove the spurs," he said.[5] Hunter was paid $5,000 for his work in this episode.

1.12 Fracas at Kiowa Flats. December 12, 1963.

Written by Carey Wilbur. Directed by Leslie H. Martinson. Executive Producer: Jack Webb. Produced by Richard M. Bluel. Filming began on November 18, 1963, and ended on November 26, 1963.

Guest stars: Kathie Browne (Meredith Nothing), Chubby Johnson (Concho), J. Pat O'Malley (Joshua C. Merry), Robert Phillips (Guard), James Best (Gotch), Art Stewart, Jean Willes (Doll Lucas), Barry Kelly (Col. Jim Sheperd), Dayton Lummis (Col. Bob Grainger), Ralph Neff (Two Finger Bill), Jonathan Hole (T. T. Teague), Hannah Landy (Kate).

Bits: Herb Vigran

Stunts: Billy Vincent, Clyde Hudkins, Byron Fromme, Buzz Henry, Louis Elias, John Harris, Clyde Howdy.

Synopsis: Houston and Taggart try to end a feud between two Civil War veterans—one from the North and the other from the South. The feud has lasted twenty years, and now Houston uses clever planning to end the feud, foil the plans of a femme fatale, and save a mail contract at the same time.

Notes: The working title for this episode was "The Stagecoach." This is the episode that marked the series' return to the tone established in the original pilot, mixing action and humor (although episode 1.14, "The Dark Madonna," was filmed earlier).

1.13 Enough Rope. December 19, 1963.

Written by Robert Vincent Wright. Directed by Irving Moore. Executive Producer: Jack Webb. Produced by Richard M. Bluel. Filming began on November 20, 1963, and ended on November 29, 1963.

Guest stars: John Dehner (Mayor Benedict Williams), Ruta Lee (Lucy Tolliver), Walter Sande (McGee), Ron Soble (Fowler), John Harmon (Crane), Tim Graham (Fred Jackson), Ed Prentiss (Burton), Steve Condit (Sammy).

Bits: Eleanor Petrie, Kenneth McDonald (Election Officer), James Chandler (Townsman), J. T. Ferguson (musician), Pat Smith (musician), Stanley West (musician), Fred Algiers (musician), and Gordon Willey (musician).

Synopsis: Houston is running for mayor, but he's running a "do-nothing" campaign over a chessboard—no campaigning, no speeches, nothing. He just keeps playing chess, mostly against Lucy Tolliver, who is supposed to be spying on Houston on the mayor's behalf. Houston's opponent, incumbent Mayor Benedict Williams, is running a smear campaign against him. By not responding to the taunts from the incumbent, Houston unnerves Williams, causing the mayor to make a costly political mistake.

Notes: Actress Ruta Lee said of Jeffrey Hunter, "He was one of the prettiest people that ever was put on the screen. God, he was gorgeous." The working title for this episode was "A Little Rope." Hunter was paid for seven days, $5,000.

1.14 The Dark Madonna. December 26, 1963.
Written by Gerry Day. Directed by John Florea. Executive Producer: Jack Webb. Produced by Joseph Dackow. Filming began September 16, 1963, and ended September 24, 1963.

Guest stars: John Seven (Rio), Vic Werber, Constance Ford (Lilly Lamont), Stacey Harris (Cliff Carteret), Phil Chambers, Penny Santon (Senora Ortega), Marianna Hill, Robert Anderson, Nick Alexander (Juan Ortega), Don Collier (Seth Warrener).

Bits: Rudolfo Hoyos, Emmett North, Bill Hickman, Frank Warren, George Robotham, Edward Astran, Herb Lytton, Byron Fromme, Tina Menard, Jo Russo, Rosa Rey, Joe Domiquez, Buzz Henry, Mae Boss.

Synopsis: Houston rides without sleep for two days at the request of a priest, who has asked for Houston's help in defending a boy who's been accused of murder. Local townspeople are determined that the boy be convicted. Houston fights a tide of resentment against himself and his client as he tries to discover the truth behind the murder.

Notes: Tom Panko, who was the assistant choreographer for the filming of *The Music Man* at Warner Brothers, was brought back to the studio to choreograph the musical number in this episode.[6] Hunter was paid $5,000 for seven days.

1.15 The Guardian. January 2, 1964.
Written by Donald S. Sanford. Directed by Robert D. Webb. Executive Producer: Jack Webb. Produced by: Richard M. Bluel. Filming began on December 2, 1963, and ended on December 9, 1963. Post-recording work done on December 16, 1963.

Guest stars: Julie Parrish (Maggie Ballard), John Archer (Adam Ballard), Greg Irvin (Robert Ballard), Robert Emhardt (Owen Judd), Rosa Turich, Ernest Sarracino, Sammy Jackson (Sodbuster), and George Lindsey.

Bits: Paul Burns, Jack Williams, Raymond Mayo, Tom Fadden, Byron Fromme.

Stunts: Byron Fromme, Rick Warwick.

Synopsis: Houston is asked by a dying man to take care of his daughter, who needs help to fight off a tyrannical rancher responsible for the man's death. The two families were fighting over water rights and a property line. Houston is appointed to be the girl's ward and must try to protect her because she wants to avenge her father's death.

Notes: Actress Julie Parrish said, "I was just a kid who had a big crush on Jeffrey Hunter. I thought his eyes were so-so wonderful. I remember being disappointed that Mr. Hunter kept to himself a lot. His behavior with me was polite, respectful, and professional."[7] The working title for this episode was "The Waterhole." Hunter was paid for seven days, $5,000.

1.16 Thy Name is Woman. January 9, 1964.

Written by Ken Pettus. Directed by William Conrad. Executive Producer: Jack Webb. Produced by: Richard M. Bluel. Filming began December 10, 1963, and ended December 16, 1963. Post-recording work done on December 23, 1963.

Guest stars: Patricia Blair (Leslie Hale), Charles Lane (Amos Riggs), Frank Ferguson (Judge Gurney), Georgia Goode (Billie Jean James), and Mary Wickes (Ida Goff).

Bits: Charles Hovath, Betty Hanna, Dick Carey (musician), Robert Clarke.

Synopsis: Houston needs help from a lady lawyer to defend a saloon hostess charged with murder, but the accused says she shot in self-defense. Houston's plan is to influence the jury by using the beautiful law partner, but his plan backfires when she starts to campaign for women's rights.

Notes: An advertisement in *The New York Times* described Houston as a "fast-talking, fast-acting lawyer in the old days of the Southwest."[8] Hunter was paid for seven days on this episode, $5,000.

1.17 The Law and Big Annie. January 16, 1964.

Written by Charles B. Smith. Directed by Charles Rondeau. Executive Producer: Jack Webb. Produced by: Richard M. Bluel. Filming began December 17, 1963, and ended December 23, 1963.

Guest stars: Charles Watts, Mary Wickes (Ida Goff), Carol Byron (Marion Carter), Norman Alden (Carlton Owens), Mickey Simpson, and Chubby Johnson (Concho).

Bits: Steve Condit, Claude Stroud, Tom Hennessey, Percy Helton.

Synopsis: Taggart dares to dream when he learns he's been given livestock in a will. He happily goes into debt to pay the freight, dreaming of the riches. Unfortunately, he learns that his inheritance is a four-ton elephant, which promptly runs up a big feed and grain bill. A decision must be made on the elephant's fate.

Notes: *The Los Angeles Times*, in reviewing this episode, said the producers were "trying to turn the series into another *Maverick* with little success thus far."[9] Hunter was paid for seven days, $5,000.

1.18 Sam's Boy. January 23, 1964.
Written by Warren Douglas. Directed by Irving J. Moore. Executive Producer: William T. Orr. Produced by: Richard M. Bluel. Filming began December 26, 1963, and ended January 3, 1964.

Guest stars: Douglas Fowley (Doc Webb), William Fawcett (Billy Rogers), Charles Seel (Henry Hicks), Frank Ferguson (Judge Gurney), Kenneth Tobey (Dan Powers), William Bryant (Cy Morgan), and Herb Vigran (Wak).

Bits: Charles Conrad, Sandy Kevin, Kenneth MacDonald (Jury Foreman), Richard Tretter (Jake Harvey), and Don Kennedy (Ike Hobbs).

Stunts: Byron Fromme, Rick Warwick, Bob Herron.

Synopsis: Three old comrades of Sam Houston want Temple Houston's help to stage a second Texas revolution, as his father had done years before. The men want to create a new Texas Republic, and want Houston to be its first president. Houston must defend them in court when they are brought up on charges of treason and inciting a revolution.

Notes: "We're getting more humor into them," Hunter said of the newest episodes. "The writers have added a tongue-in-cheek element that I personally think is good for it."[10] Hunter was paid for seven days, $5,000.

1.19 Ten Rounds for Baby. January 30, 1964.
Written by William R. Cox. Directed by William Conrad. Executive Producer: William T. Orr. Produced by: Richard M. Bluel. Filming began on January 6, 1964, and ended January 9, 1964. Post-recording work done on January 20, 1964.

Guest stars: Anne Francis (Kate Fitzpatrick), Bill Phipps (Sandy Dale), Warren Vanders, Zeme North (Baby Dale), Van Williams (Joey Baker), Dave Willock (Sandy Jackson), Frankie Van, Claude Stroud, Hal Baylor (Con Morgan).

Bits: Billy Green. Doubles: Dick Dial, Jack Williams, and Wally Brooks.

Synopsis: A local farmer, Joey Baker, wants to marry Baby, but her brothers are opposed to the marriage because the families have been feuding for years. Baker believes he needs to win the brothers over. He sees his chance when a new arrival to Lindley, Kate Fitzpatrick, announces that she is the daughter of a great boxing champion, and that she can turn him into a professional boxer. Houston, however, suspects that the match is a con.

Notes: Guest star Anne Francis, who a year later would co-star with Hunter in the Warner Brothers film *Brainstorm*, said Jeff Hunter was "a true gentleman and I thoroughly enjoyed his professionalism and courtesy."[11] Van Williams' return to the Warner Brothers lot, where he had worked for several years as a series star, was hailed in studio press releases.[12] Hunter was paid for seven days for this episode, $5,000.

1.20 The Case for William Gotch. February 6, 1964.

Written by Herman Groves. Directed by Leslie H. Martinson. Executive Producer: William T. Orr. Produced by: Richard M. Bluel. Filming began on January 10, 1964 and ended on January 17, 1964. Post-recording work was done on January 21, 1964.

Guest stars: Gordon Wescourt, Ray Danton (Martin Royale), Richard Jaeckel (Coley), Frank Ferguson (Judge Gurney), Denver Pyle (Ohineas Fallon), James Best (Gotch), Erin O'Donnell (Laura Jean), Mary Wickes (Ida Goff), and Chubby Johnson (Concho).

Bit: King Calder.

Stunt: Byron Fromme.

Synopsis: Rancher Phineas Fallen is cheated out of his property by gambler Martin Royale in a poker game. Houston launches an outrageous scheme to try to get it back for him.

Notes: In reviewing the series in January 1964, UPI writer Rick Dubrow described *Temple Houston* as a "contemporary relic" and Jeff Hunter as an "expressionless star."[13] Hunter was paid for seven days, $5,000.

1.21 A Slight Case of Larceny. February 13, 1964.

Written by Ken Pettus. Directed by William Conrad. Executive Producer: William T. Orr. Produced by: Richard M. Bluel. Filming began on January 20, 1964, and ended on January 27, 1964. Post-recording work done on January 31, 1964.

Guest stars: Vito Scotti (Pancho Blanca), Larry Ward (Harry Cobb), Chris Dark, Russell Johnson, Robert Phillips, Herb Vigran, Charles Watts (Paul Hillings), Gage Clarke, and Joe De Santis.

Bits: Robert Williams, Thomas Jackson, Carol Byron (Marion Carter), Eddie Quillan, Frank Scannell, and Ollie O' Toole.

Synopsis: A run on the bank starts, and Houston and Taggart have to come up with a scheme divert the attention of the public and put a stop to it. They enlist the aid of penniless Pancho Blanca, who brags that he was the mastermind behind a big gold robbery, and lives off the credit he establishes with the townspeople.

Notes: This was the episode that was in production when NBC decided during its January program meetings that the show would finish the season but not return for the fall. Hunter was paid for seven days, $5,000.

1.22 The Last Full Moon. February 27, 1964.

Written by Robert Sabaroff. Directed by Leslie H. Martinson. Executive Producer: William T. Orr. Produced by Richard M. Bluel. Filming began on January 28, 1964, and ended on February 2, 1964. Post-recording work was done on February 17, 1964.

Guest stars: Larry Ward (Harry Cobb), Frank Ferguson (Judge Gurney), Pilar Seurat (Bluebird), Abraham Sofaer (Chief Last Full Moon), John Alonzo (Long Maned Pony), Charles Bateman (Bowman), Charles Lane (Amos Riggs), Vaughn Taylor (Colonel Grove), Edward Colmans (Two Suns).

Bits: Greg Benedict, Rick Warwick, Louis Elias, Jack Grinnace, Alfred Ward, Bob White, Karen Noel (Dorisse), Clyde Howdy, and Maurice Wells.

Stunts: Byron Fromme, Louis Elias.

Synopsis: When the son-in-law of Chief Last Full Moon is accused of stealing a horse, the chief retains Houston as defense counsel, rather than follow the usual routine of paying off the Indian agent to set the youth free. Part of Houston's challenge from the Chief is to prove that Indian criminal cases can be settled as a matter of law, rather than through a bribe.

Notes: An ad placed by NBC in *Variety* said that Houston "built a reputation as one of the Southwest's most resourceful fighters for justice."[14] For this episode, Hunter was paid for seven days, $5,000.

1.23 The Gun That Swept the West. March 5, 1964.

Written by W. J. Voorhees. Directed by William Conrad. Executive Producer: William T. Orr. Produced by Richard M. Bluel. Filming began February 5,

1964, and ended on February 12, 1964. Hunter was recalled for an added scene on February 17, 1964.

Guest stars: John Dehner (Jed Dobbs), Chubby Johnson (Concho), Mary Wickes (Ida Goff), Sherwood Price (Dan Sheldon), Michael Pate (Nat Cramer), Henry Brandon, and William Conrad.

Bits: Ace Hudkins, John Eppers, Carol Byron, and Sailor Vincent.

Synopsis: Lovable old-timer Jed Dobbs rolls into Houston's office with his latest invention, the Dobbs Annihilator, which he's brought to town for an Army test. Houston and Taggart view the double-barreled cannon with humor and suspicion. The cannon is promptly stolen by a pair of local crooks who plan on selling it to Indians. After several close shaves, Houston and Taggart save the cannon and watch it become the town memorial.

Notes: A year before this episode was filmed, Warner Bros. was considering using an episode of Jack Elam's series *The Dakotas* as a pilot for the *Temple Houston* series. For this episode, Hunter was paid for seven days, $5,000.

1.24 Do Unto Others, Then Gallop. March 19, 1964.

Written by Ron Bishop. Directed by Leslie H. Martinson. Executive Producer: William T. Orr. Produced by Richard M. Bluel. Filming began February 12, 1964, and ended on February 19, 1964. Post-recording work was done on March 3, 1964.

Guest stars: Mary Wickes (Ida Goff), William Bramley (Gus Finney), Adam Williams, Paul Smith (Grover Clippett), Bob McQueeney (Robert Sangster), Grace Lee Whitney (Tangerine O'Shea), Claude Stroud (Murdock), Kenneth Mayer (Sam), Frank Ferguson (Judge Gurney), James Best (Gotch), and Chubby Johnson (Concho).

Bit: Rick Warwick.

Stunt: Chuck Hicks.

Synopsis: Three strangers—a drifter, a drummer, and a woman—devise a plan to frame Houston for murder for no apparent reason. When Houston is accused of murdering an unarmed man, townspeople turn against him in a "whispering" campaign. Houston demands to be heard in court to clear his name.

Notes: The working title for this episode was "Fallout at Quality Springs." Hunter was paid for seven days, $5,000.

1.25 The Town That Trespassed. March 26, 1964.

Written by Jack Turley. Directed by William Conrad. Executive Producer: William T. Orr. Produced by Richard M. Bluel. Filming began February 20, 1964, and ended on February 27, 1964. Post-recording work was done on March 3, 1964.

Guest stars: Frank Ferguson (Judge Gurney), Connie Stevens (Charity Simpson), Robert Conrad (Martin Purcell), Walter Sande (Mayor), Dave Willock (Speedy Jackson), Parley Baer (Claude Spanker), Del Jenkins (Wade), Sheldon Allman (Cutter), Martin West (Lawson), and Claude Stroud (Murdock).

Bits: Richard Collier (Mr. Huckabee), Robert Adler (Townsman).

Synopsis: A fickle young woman, Charity Simpson, and her money hungry attorney have a valid deed that demonstrates that she owns all the land the town is sitting on. Houston wines and dines the woman in an attempt to learn what's behind their scheme to lay claim to the entire town.

Notes: Writer Jack Turley said, "Hunter and Conrad were buddies."[15] Hunter was paid for seven days, $5,000.

1.26 Miss Katherine. April 2, 1964.

Written by Ken Pettus. Directed by Leslie H. Martinson. Executive Producer: William T. Orr. Produced by Richard M. Bluel. Filming began on February 27, 1964, and ended on March 4, 1964.

Guest stars: Paula Raymond (Miss Katherine), Tony Costello (Lt. Greeley), John Baer (Frank McGuire), Richard X. Slattery (Sgt. Smathers), Sammy Jackson (Wick), John Lupton (Sinclair), Simon Scott (Henry Rivers), and Donald Losby (Tommy Rivers).

Bits: Rick Warwick, Robert Phillips, Jack Coffer, Pete Kellett, and David McMahon (Doc Burgess).

Stunts: Fred Stromsoe, Clyde Hudkins, and John Amris.

Synopsis: The town spinster, Miss Katherine, loses her heart to suave Frank McGuire. She learns that he plans to rob a gold shipment, but won't tell anyone, not even when she loses her life savings.

Notes: Guest star Paula Raymond says Jack Elam taught her to play Liar's Poker between takes.[16] Hunter was paid for seven days, $5,000.

The Man from Galveston. Released December 17, 1963.

Written by Dean Reisner and Michael S. Zagaor. Directed by William Conrad. Executive Producer: Jack Webb. Produced by Michael Meshekoff.

Crew: Director of Photography: Bert Glennon; Art Director: Carl Macauley; Film Editor: Bill Wiard; Sound by: Frank Sarver; Set Decorator: William C. Kuehl; Makeup Supervisor: Gordon Bau, S.M.A.; Supervising Hair Stylist: Jean Burt Reilly, C.H.S.; Assistant Director: Victor Vallejo; Music: David Buttolph.

Cast: Jeffrey Hunter (Timothy Higgins); Preston Foster (Judge Homer Black); James Coburn (Marshal Boyd Palmer); Joanna Moore (Rita Dillard); Kevin Hagen (John Dillard); Edward Andrews (Hyde); Martin Best (Stonewall Grey); Sherwood Price (George Taggart); Ed Nelson (Cole Marteen); Grace Lee Whitney (Texas Rose).

Synopsis: Circuit court attorney Timothy Higgins has landed in Tascosa, along with the rest of the traveling court, and begins the job of taking on clients and making greetings around town. Among the townsfolk is an old girlfriend of his, Rita Crawford, now Rita Dillard, married. An old business associate from Galveston is blackmailing Rita. When the chief witness against her is killed, Rita's husband confesses to the crime to protect Rita, who actually pulled the trigger. In court, Higgins proves not only that neither Dillard murdered the witness, but that the murderer was, in fact, the man who had been blackmailing Rita.[17]

Notes: Four for Texas was among the films on the double bill with *The Man From Galveston* during the course of the latter's run. *The New York Times*, in its review, said, "Any resemblance between *The Man From Galveston* and a current television show called *Temple Houston* is far from coincidental."[18]

UNPRODUCED STORIES

Like any other television series, *Temple Houston* had a number of scripts in various stages of development that were never produced. Some story ideas never went beyond the "pitch" stage, some went as far as a lengthier story treatment, and some went to written script form. Of course, given the format change in this series, some of these scripts had to be disregarded.

What follows is a list of some of the unproduced stories for *Temple Houston*.

"Border Incident," written by John K. Butler and Lou Huston

"The County Seat Wars," written by John T. Dugan

"Court of Justice," written by John Dunkel and K. Clark

"Forty-Nine Miles to Freedom," written by Preston Wood

"Lamb to the Slaughter," written by Shimon Wincelberg

"Let There Be Law," written by William R. Cox and Jack Curtis

"Obituary for a Wayward Demagogue," written by Buckley Angell

"A Ride in the Country," written by E. M. Parsons

"Suffer Me Not to Hang," written by Jack R. Usher

"Twenty-Nine Miles to Citizenship," written by Charles B. Smith
   and Preston Wood

"Vow of Seventy-One," written by Paul Schneider

"The Wild One," written by Mort R. Lewis

There were also untitled scripts written by Harold Jack Bloom; William R. Cox and Jack Curtis; and Dean Reisner, Henry Slesar, and Lloyd Rosamond.

§

ENDNOTES

1. *Temple Houston* promotional spot, Warner Bros. Archive, University of Southern California, Los Angeles.
2. For example, see *Variety,* December 4, 1963, page 26.
3. "Jeff Hunter Gets A Sartorial Break," page 19 E.
4. Ganzer, interview
5 "Jeff Hunter Gets A Sartorial Break," page 19 E.
6. "Panko Gets *Houston* Choreograph Chore," page E 14
7. Parrish, e-mail
8. *The New York Times,* September 19, 1963.
9. "Temple Houston," *The Los Angeles Times,* page C 10
10. "New Trend in Temple Houston." *The Tuscaloosa News,* page 16.
11. Francis, letter.
12. "Williams Returns for *Temple Houston* Role," page C 16.
13. DuBrow, "Houston Falls Flat," page 40
14. *Variety,* August 7, 1963, page 36
15. Turley, interview
16. Magers, page 187
17. *The Man From Galveston,* available through Warner Home Video.
18. *The Man from Galveston, The New York Times,* 26:3

Appendix B
The Robert Taylor Show
Partial Episode Guide

This partial episode guide was assembled through an examination of the Bruce Geller Papers in the Performing Arts Special Collection at the University of California Los Angles, and by using Lee Goldberg's book *Unsold Television Pilots.*

"Pilot."
Written by Bruce Geller. Directed by Bernard Kowalski. Executive Producer: Dick Powell.

Stars: Robert Taylor (Christopher Logan) and Robert Loggia.

"A New Day Is Dying."
Written by Christopher Knopf. Directed by Bernard Kowalski. Assistant Director: Barry Crane. Dates of shooting: June 17, 18, 19, 20, 21, 24, 1963.

Star: Robert Taylor (Christopher Logan).

Guest stars: William Shatner (Karl), Carolyn Kearney (Audra), Vito Scotti (Coyema), John Anderson (Taverner), William Harlow (Jamison), Lane Bradford (Barnett), Walter Mathews (Williams), Kathleen O'Malley (Receptionist), Greg Morris (Technician), Jan Barthel (Nurse).

"Success Story."

Written by Bruce Geller. Directed by Bernard Kowalski. Assistant Director: Dave Silver. Dates of shooting: June 25, 26, 27, 28; July 1, 2, 1963.

Stars: Robert Taylor (Christopher Logan), George Segal (Nick).

Guest stars: Michael Parks (Arthur), Joanna Moore (Miss Van), John Larkin (Norman Hodgkiss), Curt Conway (Traver), Sondra Kerr (Darlene), James Maloney (Mr. Arthur), Marc Cavell (Jasper), Jeanne Appel (Anne), Kevin O'Neal (Evan).

"Hiram."

Written by Tom Seller. Directed by Barney Girard. Assistant Director: Barry Crane. Dates of shooting: July 5, 8, 9, 10, 11, 12, 1963.

Stars: Robert Taylor (Christopher Logan), George Segal (Nick).

Guest stars: Ernest Truex (Hiram), Jack Mullaney (Mort), Estelle Winwood (Amelia), Wolfe Barzell (Sam), Virginia Vincent (Molly), Harry Hickox (Judge Meechan), Hollis Irving (Ida), Pat Cardi (Joey), Bruno Della Santina (Morelli), Marla Craig (Female Clerk).

"Shadows Of The World Appear."

Written by Lawrence Edward Watkin. Directed by Bernard Kowalski. Assistant Director: Dave Silver. Dates of shooting: July 15, 16, 17, 18, 19, 22, 1963.

Stars: Robert Taylor (Christopher Logan), George Segal (Nick).

Guest stars: Lawrence Dobkin (Jacob Miller), Luana Anders (Katri Miller), Peter Helm (Carl Miller), Bert Freed (John Baumgartner), Peggy Webber (Mrs. Baumgartner), Howard Caine (Franklin Potts), Vernon Rich (Kurtz).

§

Appendix C
Unrealized Jeffrey Hunter Projects

J effrey Hunter's name was connected with many film and television projects during the course of his career, many of which were never made, or made with other performers. Like the history connecting *The Robert Taylor Show* and *Temple Houston*, this list represents an intriguing "What if" aspect on Hunter's career in film and television, and some of these near misses are what led the actor to *Temple Houston*.

Consider—Jeffrey Hunter, in the spring of 1966, signed a contract for work in two low budget films with producer Sidney Pink. That deal was the result of a frustrating three year cycle in which the actor had seen *Temple Houston* rushed into production, leading to failure; had starred in an NBC television pilot written by Eric Ambler that didn't go; and had suffered near-misses in projects involving no less than John Ford, Samuel Fuller, and Stanley Kubrick. Instead, Hunter found himself in Spain starring in *A Witch Without a Broom* and *The Christmas Kid*.

"Sometimes this career has many bitter moments," Hunter said in 1968. "You really need to have…willpower and patience to wait for your opportunity, and many times it never comes."[1]

This list was compiled from a variety of sources, including articles from The Associated Press and United Press International in local newspapers; articles in trade publications such as *Variety*, *Box Office*, and *The Hollywood Reporter*; and newspaper accounts.

The Pony Soldier

Tyrone Power eventually starred in this Western at 20th Century-Fox, but the producers had Hunter in mind for the film because the script called for a young lead, something Power did not represent in 1952.

The Big Game

Director Francis Lyon mentioned Hunter as a possibility for this proposed film about a college football coach in 1957.

Appointment with Danger

This was a film Hunter was making when he was stricken with hepatitis in 1958 and the part had to be recast. The working title for the film was *If I Should Die.*

Secret of Bat Canyon

Marion Hargrove wrote this suspense story for Thunderbird Pictures in 1958 and Hunter was mentioned as the lead.

Let My Heart Be Broken

Hunter was mentioned as the lead for this projected 20th Century-Fox film based on the experiences of Dr. Robert Pierce, who founded World Vision when he learned of the plight of GI orphans in Korea.

Three for the Road

Hunter purchased the rights to this Winston Schiller comedy in 1959, but couldn't launch the film. The story concerned three people hitchhiking from New York to Hollywood because they want a career in movies.

The Golden Hoard

Hunter's production company also purchased the rights to this story by Clay Fisher, an adventure about the Spanish main.

The Sea Nymph

Hunter's name popped up in connection with this Eddie Alperson film with Bob Strauss and Terry Moore in 1959.

The Horse Soldiers

Director John Ford wanted Hunter for this Civil War drama starring John Wayne, released in 1959.

Walls Come Tumbling Down

In 1959, Jan Sterling said she was trying to sign Hunter to star opposite her in this picture, to be produced by her husband in France, Holland, and West Germany.

The Best of Everything

Hunter was listed among the possibles for this Fox soap opera, released in 1959.

Leo Lax film—*Checkmate* television series

Hunter was offered the starring role in a European film based on the life of Emperor Constantine I being proposed by producer Leo Lax. At the same time, Hunter was considering an offer to star in the television series *Checkmate*, created by Eric Ambler. The decision, which Hunter said was a hard one, was made for him when he was offered the lead in *King of Kings*.

Equitable Life Theatre

Hunter starred in this unsold, unaired pilot for a series based on historical events at the nation's colleges and universities. It was shot in 1961. Hunter played Father Edward Sorin in this drama about the founding of The University of Notre Dame.

Captain Kidd

Producer Sam Bronston tried to get this adventure film mounted in the early 1960s, but was unsuccessful. He wanted Hunter for the lead.

Magellan

Based on the explorer's life, this was another Sam Bronston film proposal. The production costs and less than expected box office returns on other Bronston films, such as *Circus World* and *The Fall of the Roman Empire*, forced the producer to scale back many of his plans.

Tent of the Wicked

Based on a Robert Switzer novel about a Latin-American dictator, this film idea was pitched in 1961 by writer Charles Lang and producer-director William F. Claxton. Hunter and Van Heflin were sought for lead roles.

A Machine for Chuparosa

This project represents one of the most frustrating near misses in Hunter's career, and a personal disappointment for the actor. He talked about this film repeatedly; it was a project that had a green light in late 1961 and early 1962 under producer Hall Bartlett, but it fell through each time. The story focused on a soldier of fortune trying to get a tractor for a starving village in Mexico so the villagers can grow their own food.

Antelope and Enterprise

In 1961, Hunter purchased the rights to this historical novel by Anthony Bevan, but never managed to get the film produced. Bevan had been a consultant on the Roman military on *King of Kings*, and authored two books on the Roman Empire.

Baby Talk

Hunter would have played the lead role, that of a comedy-con man, in 1961.

Knights of Charlemagne

Leo Lux wanted Hunter for the lead role in this film, proposed for a July 1961 start. Hunter would have played Roland, a major romantic figure of the time who helped Charlemagne invade Spain in 778.

The Young Doctors

Hunter read the script for this 1961 drama based on an Arthur Hailey novel about a medical hospital. Doubtless the actor would have enjoyed working with Fredric March, one of the great American actors.

Last Plane to Shanghai

In 1962, Hunter said he had read this novel by Richard Tregoskis about a disillusioned journalist in Shanghai and would love to play the lead in a film based on the book.

The Caretakers

Hunter was cast in a lead role in this drama, but when actor Robert Stack said he was willing to put some of his own money into financing the film, he was in and Hunter was out.

PT 109

Hunter was among the actors who did a screen test for the role of Lt. John F. Kennedy in this 1963 film, but President Kennedy selected Cliff Robertson for the part instead.

The Last of the Mohicans

Hunter's involvement in this Western, to be produced by a production team from Germany and Spain, was announced in 1963.

The Last Hundred Hours

As early as December 1962, Hunter was talking about being in this film. Announced in November 1963 for an early spring 1964 start, this film boasted a screenplay by Stanley Kubrick and Robert Adams and dealt with the collapse of the Nazi Army in the last days of World War II in northern Italy. Gerd Oswald was set to direct. The film was delayed but announced again in 1965, with location work to be done in Spain and Italy and interiors in Rome and Madrid. Unfortunately, the film was never made and remains one of Kubrick's unproduced scripts. The "discovery" of the "lost" script was announced in 1999.

Cheyenne Autumn

Though cast as one of the five leads in John Ford's final Western (initially titled *The Long Flight*), Hunter had to bow out of this 1964 release when *Temple Houston* went into production. The film started shooting in October, making it impossible for Hunter to participate. Being visible in this film would have been a nice boost for the actor in 1964, after the cancellation of *Temple Houston*.

The Secret

Hunter was to play a naval officer in this jewel heist melodrama, to be filmed in Spain in 1964.

My Blood Runs Cold

Warner Bros. had originally cast Hunter in this film as part of his WB contract, but as the film went into production in the fall of 1964, the studio and the actor agreed that he would not star in the film. He was cast in *Brainstorm* instead.

Battle Royale

Hunter and Robert Wagner were the finalists for the lead in this espionage drama written by Sam Fuller, and Hunter won the part. The film was scheduled to go into production in several European locations in the summer of 1965 with Gerry O'Hara directing and Curt Jurgens and Shirley Eaton listed as guest stars, but was never made. The well-respected Fuller really liked this script and fifteen years later was still talking about his hopes for making the film.

Journey into Fear

A television adventure-espionage series proposed by Eric Ambler and executive producer William Dozier, this pilot was produced in late 1965 and seemed a sure thing for NBC's 1966–67 schedule. NBC changed its mind and never put the series into production. Indeed, the pilot itself, co-starring Sally Ann Howes, was never even shown on television, although many similar unsold pilots were seen as episodes of the various network anthology series of the day.

Strange Portrait

This film was actually completed in late 1965 and early 1966 in Hong Kong, but was lost in a fire. It was the first all-English language movie made in Hong Kong. Hunter starred as an American ex-pat in Hong Kong, trying to heist jewels from an elderly woman. He becomes permanently trapped in her secret vault when the woman, who is insane, shuts him inside.

Fickle Finger of Fate

Hunter signed a two-picture deal with producer Sidney Pink in 1966, and was originally cast in this film, about an American tourist who helps Spanish police find a stolen religious candlestick.

Five Against Kansas

A Civil War drama which was to have been filmed in 1967, co-starring Tippi Hedren and John Saxon.

King Gun

Hunter was connected with this film, on and off, for the last two years of his life. The production schedule for *Viva America* prevented him from taking part when the film finally went into production in 1969; it was eventually released as *The Gatling Gun*.

The Brady Bunch

Hunter lobbied heavily for the role of Mike Brady as this situation comedy was being developed for network television. He did screen tests and interviewed twice for the role. Given how children took to the actor, one can easily picture him in this show, especially the first season, when the children were younger. Unfortunately for Hunter, producer Sherwood Schwartz felt he was too good-looking for the part; Lloyd Schwartz, the producer's son, preferred Hunter for the role.

All the Way to the Bank

Hunter was signed to play the lead in this film, announced in 1967 and to be produced by Milton H. Lehr of Continental Studios. Filming was cancelled just before it was scheduled to start in Miami that August.

Seven Crosses to Sundown

This comedy-drama set after the Civil War was announced in trade papers in May 1969, co-starring Hunter and Rory Calhoun. Filming was set to begin in early June.

Band of Brothers

At the time of his death, Hunter was talking about appearing in a Korean War drama starring Vince Edwards, with shooting possible for August.

§

ENDNOTE

1. Hernandez, pages 48-51.

Bibliography

ARTICLES

"Actor Jeffrey Hunter Dies of Injuries; Fall Believed Cause." *The Los Angeles Times*, May 28, 1969.

Adams, Val. "32 New TV Shows Scheduled for Fall Season." *The New York Times*, January 29, 1964.

Arneel, Gene. "Metro Sales Tactics Reversed on Kings; Now Foresees It as 'Second-Wind' Blockbuster." *Variety,* May 9, 1962.

Bawden, James. "Elam is Good at Being Bad and It's Won Him a Starring Role." *The Montreal Gazette,* October 27, 1979.

"Big Scale Friendship Seen on 'Temple Houston' Lot." *The Tuscaloosa News*, January 26, 1964.

"Big Picture- Maker Samuel Bronston Based in Dallas for Comeback Drive." *Box Office*, February 26, 1973.

"Bits of Show Business." *The Milwaukee Journal*, August 11, 1965.

"Bluel to Produce 'Houston' TV Series." *The Los Angeles Times*, November 26, 1963.

Buck, Jerry. "Jack Elam's Image Has Changed." *The Pittsburgh-Post Gazette*, July 30, 1974.

Buck, Jerry. "Jack Elam: Monstrously Fun." *The Wilmington Morning Star.* September 19, 1979.

Calhoun, Sue Rhodes. "Bottom Line on a Top Heavy." *The Los Angeles Times.* May 29, 1977.

Crowther, Bosley. "King of Kings." *The New York Times,* October 12, 1961.

Denton, Charles. "New TV Trend is Strictly for Laughs!" *The Hartford Courant,* January 5, 1964.

"Dick Powell Dies After Cancer Fight." *The Sarasota Journal*, January 3, 1963.

"Did Storylines Kill Taylor Show?" *Television Age*, August 5, 1963.

"Do You Remember Warner Bros.' Temple Houston." *Western Clippings*, No. 16, March/April 1997.

DuBrow, Rick. "Houston Falls Flat." *The Pittsburgh Press,* January 17, 1964.

DuBrow, Rick. "Temple Falling to Ruins." *The News Dispatch*, January 17, 1964.

Dutton, Walt. "Lawyer Houston's Case Loses Punch in Pinch." *The Los Angeles Times*, September 21, 1963.

"Elam Killed Again by Jimmy Stewart." *Hawkins County-Post Magazine*, March 21, 1968.

"Everybody a Bible Student: Liked the Book Better than the Pic." *Variety*, October 18, 1961.

"An Eyebrow Lifted, a Show Dropped." *Broadcasting,* July 22, 1963.

Fanning, Win. "Villain Jack Elam to Join the Good Guys." *The Pittsburg Post-Gazette,* December 4, 1962.

"Film Report: Distribution World Wide." *Television Age,* September 16, 1963.

"Film Report: Production." *Television Age,* November 25, 1963.

Finnigan, Joseph. "Actor Hunter to Have Eyes of Texas on Him." *The Miami Herald*, March 26, 1963.

Finnigan, Joseph. "Bob Taylor Ready, Eager to Begin New TV Series." *The Hartford Courant*, December 16, 1962.

Finnigan, Joseph. "Ex- Heavy Jack Elam Most Unusual Marshal." *The Hartford Courant*, October 6, 1963.

"Frontier Lawyer Had to be Colorful." *The Hartford Courant*, December 22, 1963.

Gardner, Paul. "Order in the Court! The TV Lawyer Wants to Speak." *The New York Times*, February 16, 1964.

Gould, Jack. "Nielsens Show a Loss for CBS." *The New York Times*, October 28, 1963.

Gould, Jack. "Hillbillies Lead in Nielsen Study." *The New York Times*, October 29, 1963.

Gould, Jack. "TV: Ratings of the Autumn Premieres." *The New York Times*, October 30, 1963.

Gould, Jack. "NBC- A Video Mystery." *The New York Times,* October 31, 1963.

Grant, Hank. "Bob Taylor Back on TV With Exciting News Series." *The Hartford Courant*, July 7, 1963.

Grant, Hank. "Jeff Hunter Breaks Hollywood Jinx." *The Chicago Tribune*, January 11, 1964.

Grant, Hank. "Robert Vaughn Wants to Quit 'Lieutenant.'" *The Evening Independent*, St. Petersburg, October 29, 1963.

Grant, Hank. "The TV News Beat." *The Hartford Courant,* October 20, 1963.

Hartung, Philip T. "Screen: What is Truth." *Commonweal,* November 13, 1961.

Hefferman, Harold. "Jeff Hunter Plods Along Successfully." *The Toledo Blade,* August 23, 1963.

Heimer, Mel. "For George, Television is Back to School." *The Rochester Sentinel,* December 14, 1967.

Hernandez, Vladimir G. "Jeffrey Hunter: 42 Years and 45 Movies Filmed." *CINEavance,* no. 181, April 20, 1968.

Hoffman, Nellie. "I Prefer to be a Good, Stable Actor Than a Fleeting Star." *El Sol y las Estrellas,* #165, June 1969.

Hopper, Hedda. "Bob Taylor a VIP? Nobody Asked Him." *The Los Angeles Times,* January 17, 1963.

Hopper, Hedda. "Bruno, the Sexy Banjo Player." *The Chicago Tribune Magazine,* November 22, 1964.

Hopper, Hedda. "Foy Will Film 'Seeds of Madrid.'" *The Los Angeles Times,* January 13, 1966.
Humphrey, Hal. "The 10 Worst TV Wastelanders." *The Los Angeles Times,* December 29, 1963.

Hunter, Jeffrey. "Actor's Choice." *Films and Filming,* April 1962.

"Hunter's Paradise." *Movieland,* November 1963.

"Hunter to Star in Anthology Premiere." *The Los Angeles Times,* February 22, 1961.

"Jack Elam Has Been Frightening Audiences For Years." *The Day,* September 15, 1979.

"Japanese Net Buys 'Houston' in TV Package." *The Dallas Morning News,* August 27, 1963.

"Jeff Hunter Defied 'Jinx' in Film Role." *Chicago's Sunday American*, TV Roundup, May 31, 1964.

"Jeff Hunter Gets a Sartorial Break." *The Hartford Courant*, December 15, 1963.

"Jeff Hunter Signs Movie, TV Contract." *The Miami News*, April 21, 1963.

"Jeffrey Hunter, Film Actor, is Dead." *The New York Times*, May 28, 1969.

"Jeffrey Hunter in 'Flight.'" *The Hollywood Reporter*, July 15, 1963.

"Jeffrey Hunter Unlike Real-Life Temple Houston." *The Dallas Morning News*. January 15, 1964.

"King of Kings." *Variety*, December 31, 1960.

Johnson, Erskine. "Filming of 'King of Kings' Has Story Inside the Story." *The Florence Times*, November 26, 1962.

Kleiner, Dick. "Hunter: TV Needs Dictators." *The Florence Times*, August 17, 1965.

Kleiner, Dick. "Loggia Knows How to Fail by Really Trying." *The Tuscaloosa News*, July 25, 1964.

Kleiner, Dick. "Lucked into Acting, Says Robert Taylor." *The Tuscaloosa News*, March 17, 1963.

Landry, Robert J. "King of Kings." *Variety*, October 11, 1961.

Lowry, Cynthia. "Jack Webb Finds Spot in Fall TV for Lawyer Show." *The Miami News*, August 22, 1963.

Lowry, Cynthia. "Some Fall Shows Already on the Ropes." *Hopkinsville Kentucky New Era*. October 7, 1963.

Lowry, Cynthia. "Temple Houston Could Be Guilty." *Kentucky New Era*, September 20, 1963.

MacMinn, Aleene. "Hunter Answers Skeptics." *The Los Angeles Times*, October 13, 1963.

Martin, Douglas. "Jack Elam, Lazy-Eyed Movie Villain, is Dead." *The New York Times*, October 23, 2003.

Merlman, Richard M. "Power and Community in Television." *The Journal of Popular Culture*, Summer, 1968.

Molloy, Paul. "NBC Will Junk Big-Name Shows." *The Los Angeles Times*, January 30, 1964.

Mosby, Wade H. "Showbiz." *The Milwaukee Journal*, July 28, 1963.

"Movies, New TV Series Set by Robert Taylor." *The Deseret News*, March 27, 1963.

"NBC Explains Dumping of TV Series." *The Los Angeles Times*, July 20, 1963.

"New Trend in Temple Houston." *The Tuscaloosa News*, January 12, 1964.
O' Flaherty, Terrence. "How Green Was My Money." *The San Francisco Chronicle*, September 19, 1963.

O' Flaherty, Terrence. "Return of Dum-De-Dum-Dum." *The San Francisco Chronicle*, November 21, 1963.

"Panko Gets 'Houston' Choreograph Chore." *The Los Angeles Times*, October 2, 1963.

Parsons, Louella O. "Jeffrey Hunter." *The Los Angeles Herald Examiner*. October 1, 1961.

Phillips, Lee. "Silver-Tongued Temple Houston, the Son of Sam, Practiced Law and Practiced With a Gun, Too." *Wild West*, February 1997.

"The Picture of a Classic Villain." *TV Guide*. June 1, 1963.

Porter, Reed. "Temple Houston: 'The Twisted Rope.'" *The Hollywood Reporter*, September 23, 1963.

"Preview of Today's TV." *The Los Angeles Times*, January 16, 1964.

Pruess, Lucile. "Blue Eyed Bandit in Senorita Land." *The Milwaukee Journal*, October 4, 1964.

Purcelli, Marion. "Acting is a Craft, Not an Escape." *The Chicago Tribune*, March 30, 1963.

Rose, Reginald. "Law, Drama, Criticism." *Television Quarterly*, Vol. III, Issue 4, fall 1964.

Scheurer, Philip K. "Christus Portrayal No Longer 'Types.'" *The Los Angeles Times*, January 22, 1965.

Schmitt, Joan. "Male Call." *Los Angeles Citizen News*, January 30, 1965.

Scott, Vernon. "'Robert Taylor Show' Off Before It's On." *The Beaver County Times*, July 27, 1963.

"Segal on TV." *The Gadsden Times*, July 13, 1963.

"Sheila Graham's Hollywood." *The Edmonton Journal.* February 7, 1962.

Shepard, Richard F. "NBC- TV Cancels Series of Dramas." *The New York Times*, July 18, 1963.

Shull, Richard. "Jack Elam Set for ABC Series." *Waycross Journal-Herald,* August 3, 1974.

"Sign Hunter to Contract." *The Ottawa Citizen,* Entertainment, March 23, 1963.

"$ign of the Cross." *Time,* October 27, 1961.

Smith, Cecil. "After Rites, Tonight's Bright." *The Los Angeles Times*, October 23, 1963.

Smith, Cecil. "Better Late Than Never for Webb." *The Los Angeles Times*, August 12, 1963.

Smith, Cecil. "High, Low Notes from Videoland." *The Los Angeles Times*, July 31, 1963.

Smith, Cecil. "Jack Webb Tells Plans for 5 New TV Shows." *The Los Angeles Times*, March 14, 1963.

Smith, Cecil. "New Shows Play Russian Roulette." *The Los Angeles Times*, August 9, 1963.

Spiro, J.D. "Chills, Thrills, and Romance." *The Milwaukee Journal*, September 1, 1963.

Spiro, J.D. "Happy in Hollywood." *The Milwaukee Journal*, July 4, 1965.

Spiro, J.D. "TV Plum Eludes Robert Taylor, Falls in Hands of Jeffrey Hunter." *The Milwaukee Journal*, July 26, 1963.

Stern, Harold. "Robert Taylor One Actor Not Afraid to Speak Up." *The Hartford Courant*, August 16, 1964.

Stewart, Scott. "Jack Elam: It Pays to be Hateful." *The Beaver County Times*, August 13, 1979.

"Taylor to Serve as Executive." *The Star-News*, Wilmington, North Carolina, June 6, 1963.

"Temple Houston," *The Los Angeles Times*, January 16, 1964.

"Temple Houston." *Radio Times*, October 15, 1964.

"Temple Houston." *TV Guide*, program listings, 1963- 1964.

"Temple Houston." *Variety*, September 25, 1963.

"Ten Push-Ups and I Simmer Down." *TV Guide*, January 11, 1964.

"Ten Writers Plotting NBC Legal Series." *The Los Angeles Times*, August 13, 1963.

Terry, Clifford. "Hunter Avoids Typing With Varied Roles." *The Chicago Tribune*, April 9, 1967.

"The Man From Galveston." *The New York Times*, January 23, 1964, 26:3.

"The Man From Galveston." *Variety*, January 15, 1964.

"The Picture of a Classic Villain." *TV Guide*, June 1, 1963.

Thomas, Bob. "Hollywood." *The Daytona Beach Morning Journal*, October 20, 1961.

Thomas, Bob. "Jeffrey Hunter to Play Jesus in 'King of Kings.'" *The Owosso Argus-Press*, April 28, 1960.

Thomas, Bob. "Shift to Comedy May Save Show." *Hopkinsville Kentucky New Era,* December 21, 1963.

Tolbert, Frank X. "Temple Houston's Family Speaks Up." *The Dallas Morning News*, August 25, 1963.

"Travel Logs." *The Hollywood Reporter*, July 23, 1963.

"TV Scout Reports." *The Southeast Missourian*, October 17, 1963.

"TV Teletype: Hollywood." *TV Guide*, June 28, 1963.

"TV Teletype: Hollywood." *TV Guide*, July 13, 1963.

"TV Teletype: Hollywood." *TV Guide*, August 3, 1963.

Walsh, Moira. "Christ or Credit Card?" *America*, October 21, 1961.

West, Dick. "Jack Elam Rather Perturbed Over TV Role as Good Guy." *Williamson Daily News,* December 6, 1962.

Williams, Edward Bennett. "The High Cost of Television's Courtroom." *Television Quarterly*, Vol. III, Issue 4, fall 1964.

"Williams Returns for *Temple Houston* Role." *The Los Angeles Times,* January 13, 1964.

Wolters, Larry. "Temple Houston Tale Has Got It: Violence." *The Chicago Tribune*, September 20, 1963.

BOOKS

Anderson, Lindsay. *About John Ford*. London, England: Plexus Publishing, 1985.

Anderson, Christopher. *Hollywood TV: The Studio System in the Fifties*. Austin, Texas: University of Texas Press, 1994.

Asherman, Allen. *The Star Trek Interview Book*. New York, New York: Pocket Books, 1988.

Brooks, Tim, and Earle Marsh. *The Complete Directory to Primetime Network and Cable TV Shows*, 6th ed. New York, New York: Ballantine, 1995.

Burlingame, Jon. *TV's Biggest Hits*. New York, New York: Schirmer Books, 1996.

Buscombe, Edward. *The BFI Companion to the Western*. New York, New York: Atheneum, 1988.

Engel, Joel. *Gene Roddenberry: The Myth and the Man Behind Star Trek*. New York, NY: Hyperion, 1996.

Fraser, George MacDonald. *The Hollywood History of the World*. New York, New York: Fawcett Columbine, 1989.

Fitzgerald, Michael G., with Boyd Magers. *Ladies of the Western*. Jefferson, North Carolina: McFarland Publishers Inc., 2010.

Ford, Dan. *Pappy: The Life of John Ford*. Englewood Cliffs, New Jersey: Prentice Hall, 1979.

Goldberg, Lee. *Unsold Television Pilots, 1955 through 1988*. Jefferson, North Carolina: McFarland Publishers, Inc., 1990.

Gross, Edward, and Mark Altman. *Great Birds of the Galaxy*. East Meadow, New York: Image Publishing, 1992.

Gross, Edward. *Trek Classic: 25 Years Later*. East Meadow, New York: Image Publishing, 1991.

Hayde, Michael J. *My Name's Friday*. Nashville, Tennessee: Cumberland House, 2001.

Hunter, J. Marvin, and Noah H. Rose. *The Album of Gunfighters*. 1951.

Inman, David. *The TV Encyclopedia*. New York, New York: Perigee Books, 1991.

Jarvis, Robert M., and Paul R. Joseph. *Prime Time Law*. Durham, North Carolina: Carolina Academic Press, 1998.

Kennedy, Burt. *Hollywood Trail Boss*. New York, New York: Boulevard Books, 1997.

Knopf, Christopher. *Will the Real Me Please Stand Up*. Albany, Georgia: Bear Manor Media, 2010.

Lentz, Harris M. *Television Westerns Episode Guide: All United States Series 1949-1996*. Jefferson, North Carolina: McFarland Publishers, Inc, 1997.

Magers, Boyd, with Michael G. Fitzgerald. *Westerns Women*. Jefferson, North Carolina: McFarland Publishers Inc., 2004.

Nunn, Michael. *The Stories Behind the Scenes of the Great Film Epics*. Watford: Illustrated Publications Co. Ltd., 1982.

Schwartz, Sherwood, with Lloyd J. Schwartz. *Brady, Brady, Brady*. Philadelphia, Pennsylvania: Running Press, 2010.

Shirley, Glenn. *Temple Houston: Lawyer with a Gun*. Norman, Oklahoma: University of Oklahoma Press, 1980.

Shulman, Arthur, and Roger Youman. *The Golden Age of Television*. New York, New York: Bonanza Books, 1979.

Solow, Herbert F., with Robert H. Justman. *Inside Star Trek: The Real Story.* New York, New York: Pocket Books, 1996.

Stempel, Tom. *Storytellers to the Nation: A History of American Television Writing.* New York, New York: Continuum, 1992.

Summers, Neil. *The Official TV Western Book*, vol. 2. Vienna, West Virginia: Old West Publishing, 1989.

Terrace, Vincent. *The Complete Encyclopedia of Television Programs, 1947- 1976.* South Brunswick, NJ and New York, New York: A.S. Barnes and Company, 1979.

Wayne, Jane Ellen. *Robert Taylor.* New York, New York: St. Martin's Press, 1987.

West, Richard. *Television Westerns.* Jefferson, North Carolina: McFarland Publishers, Inc., 1987.

White. Patrick J. *The Mission Impossible Dossier.* New York, New York: Avon Books, 1991.

Whitfield, Stephen E., and Gene Roddenberry. *The Making of Star Trek.* New York, New York: Ballantine, 1968.

Yoggy, Gary A. *Riding the Video Range: The Rise and Fall of the Western on Television.* Jefferson, North Carolina: McFarland Publishers, Inc.

ARCHIVES

Bruce Geller Papers. Performing Arts Special Collections, University of California Los Angeles, Los Angeles, CA.

Eric Ambler Collection. Howard Gotlieb Archival Research Center, Boston University, Boston, MA.

James Warner Bellah Collection. Howard Gotlieb Archival Research Center, Boston University, Boston, MA.

John Ford Papers. Lilly Library, Indiana University, Bloomington, Indiana.

Temple Houston Series Collection. Warner Brothers Archives, University of Southern California, Los Angeles, CA.

University of Notre Dame Archives, Hesburgh Library, Notre Dame, Indiana.

WEB SITES

BFI Film and TV Database, www.bfi.org.uk/filmtvinfo/ftvdb

The Classic TV Archive, http://ctva.biz/index.htm

Doug Abbott Collection, www.westerntvphotos.com

The Internet Movie Database, www.imdb.com

Leonard Nimoy interview, The Archive of American Television, interviewed by Karen Herman, November 2, 2000, www.emmytvlegends.org

Worldcat, www.worldcat.org

OTHER SOURCES

Mary Ann Anderson, telephone interview. December 6, 1994.

Anne Francis, letter to the author. May 26, 1999.

James Best, e-mail correspondence with author. December 29, 2010.

Robert Douglas, letter to the author. August 8, 1997.

Charles B. Fitzsimons, telephone interview. January 10, 1994.

Alvin Ganzer, telephone interview. May 29, 1997.

King of Kings. New York: Metro-Goldwyn-Mayer/Samuel Bronston Productions, Inc. Promotional materials.

Christopher Knopf, e-mail correspondence with the author. January 17, 2011.

France Nuyen, telephone interview. July 18, 1997.

Julie Parrish, e-mail correspondence with the author. May 19, 1997.

Joseph Pevney, telephone interview. August 4, 1997.

Mai Tai Sing, e-mail correspondence with author. May 21, 1998.

Jeffrey Stone, e-mail correspondence with author. February 3, 2009

George Takei, personal interview. Hyannis, MA. August 21, 1992.

Jack Turley, letter to the author. April 1, 1994.

Jack Turley, telephone interview. March 23, 1994.

Van Williams, telephone interview. January 11, 2011.

Marie Windsor, telephone interview. May 15, 1997.

ADDITIONAL SCRIPTS

Turley, Jack. "The Town that Trespassed," courtesy of Jack Turley.

Turley, Jack. "The Twisted Rope," from a story by James Warner Bellah, courtesy of Jack Turley.

Personal Name Index

About the Author

Glenn A. Mosley is Director of Broadcasting and member of the faculty at the University of Idaho's School of Journalism and Mass Media. His first book, *Henry Fonda and The Deputy: The Film and Stage Star and His TV Western,* was also published by BearManor Media.

CPSIA information can be obtained at www.ICGtesting.com
Printed in the USA
266861BV00003B/226/P